ROWING AFTER THE W

Rowing After the White Whale

A crossing of the Indian Ocean by hand

In which I detail our preparations for, and execution of, the first unsupported pairs row across the Indian Ocean, including an account of our capsize and death-defying swim to shore, many factual deviations about various wildlife we saw, the history of ocean rowing and occasional references to, and comparisons with, whaling and *Moby Dick*, a book we had on board and which found its way into our hearts.

JAMES ADAIR

This edition first published in Great Britain in 2015 by
Polygon, an imprint of Birlinn Ltd
West Newington House
10 Newington Road
Edinburgh
EH9 1QS
www.polygonbooks.co.uk

First published in 2013

ISBN: 978 1 84697 327 7

eBook ISBN: 978 0 85790 599 4

British Library Cataloguing-in-Publication Data
A catalogue record for this book is available
on request from the British Library

Typeset in Great Britain by Palimpsest Book Production Limited,
Falkirk, Stirlingshire
Printed and bound by Clays Ltd, St Ives plc

For Ben, thank you for sharing the adventure

And for Tory, thank you for believing me

Contents

Prologue
17.15, 14 August 2011 (Day 116)

Now we're going to die, I thought as the wall of white water came thundering towards us. My heart thumped as my body started furiously pumping adrenaline in anticipation of the impact.

For a moment the sea in front of the wave looked still and pure, so peaceful and blue in contrast with the white rolling mass that was now seconds away. But already the flat in front of the wave was being disturbed and soiled by spitting shards of tumbling white water. The noise grew suddenly louder, from a rumbling hiss to a raging thunder as the turmoil of water reached us.

Now we really are, actually, definitely, after all of this, after everything, going to die, I thought. *Typical.* As for words, the only one I could manage in time, the only one that seemed appropriate, was: 'Shit!'

I took a deep breath.

The wave hit us with a violent, sickening crash and everything went black.

PART ONE

The Build-up

1 Beginnings

> 'Whenever I find myself growing grim about the
> mouth; whenever it is a damp, drizzly November in
> my soul . . . and especially whenever my hypos get
> such an upper hand of me, that it requires a strong
> moral principle to prevent me from deliberately
> stepping into the street, and methodically knocking
> people's hats off – then, I account it high time to
> get to sea as soon as I can.'
>
> Herman Melville, *Moby Dick*

It's no surprise that Ben and I decided to row an ocean when
you consider our dissolute characters and unremarkable
circumstances during the dark November of 2004. We had
graduated from the University of St Andrews six months
before and were struggling to readjust to city life. After four
years of fun and games we had given up the freedom and
fresh air of Scotland for the trudging London commute
and a flat in which we, and the mice we lived with, were
regularly plunged into darkness as the pay-as-you-go electricity
ran out yet again. I had been talked into doing a law course,
which I wasn't enjoying, but Ben had suffered a worse fate. He
was selling fully integrated accounting software in Lewisham.
It's not hard to see why we started dreaming of a big adventure
and, as complete ocean novices, we settled on rowing the Pacific,
which is of course the biggest of all the oceans.

The Pacific – the very word seemed to summon up the
wide expanse of ocean, the equatorial sun beating down on

the two of us hauling in another massive tuna for lunch. Yes, the daydreams were unrealistic but they were alluring and they had us hooked. Every time I rode the 59 bus or the tube, crammed in, standing again, wedged between ashen-faced salary man and morbidly obese tourist, accompanied by the sound of an aggressive track-suited mother chiding her toddler or the ramblings of some unwashed nutter; every time my mind would drift off to sea, to a place where you couldn't see another human being in any direction. Space, solitude and silence, these were the things I craved – and, of course, a massive skive off work. Back in our flat we'd discuss the mad scheme over shepherd's pie and red wine.

'We really have to do the rowing, no matter what.'

'Yeah, definitely.'

'I'm not kidding Ben, we have to get out there as soon as we can.'

'I'm ready now.'

'No but really, we should really do it.'

'Stop worrying Adair, we both know when we get out there I'll end up doing all the rowing.'

'Will you be bringing those mustard coloured corduroys of yours?'

'Absolutely, will you be bringing your riding boots?'

'There's really nothing funny about my riding boots, they have a specific purpose, what's the purpose of your mustard coloured corduroys?'

'Primarily to keep me warm but their secondary purpose is to make me look good, very good.'

'Every weekend you look sillier than the last, also you're beginning to look quite, how do I put this delicately, fat.'

'I have no time to eat properly, you can't imagine what sort of demands selling fully integrated accounting software packages can put on a man's body, they say most people burn out by the time they hit twenty five.'

'Well, if we run out of food when we're in the middle of the ocean I think it's quite clear who'll be eating who.'

'Yes, in that scenario I will be over-powering and eating you.'

'In which case you'll just have eaten one of your two friends.'

'Let's face it, if we go missing at sea very few people are going to notice we're gone.'

'That's true.'

Soon our nightly chats became more serious, we *would* row the Pacific, it wasn't just empty chat, we *had* to row the Pacific, or it would become another dream that slowly slips away. We knew that a lot of people had rowed the Atlantic, on the well-travelled route from the Canaries to the Caribbean, but we wanted to do something different, something bigger, newer, more dangerous. And so we plumped for the Pacific. Our casual research showed that one man had rowed the South Pacific solo without stopping and two pairs had done it in legs. Fine, *we* would be the first pair to row the South Pacific without stopping.

2 Interim

'Always do sober what you said you'd do drunk.
That will teach you to keep your mouth shut.'
Ernest Hemingway

In 2005 we left London and went our separate ways. Ben made the logical step from fully integrated accounting software salesman in Lewisham to logistics and freight forwarding manager in Uganda (having grown up in Kenya, he was basically going home). I eventually got a job in journalism as editor of the *Alderney Journal*, probably the smallest paid-for newspaper in the world, serving a mere two thousand souls on the island of Alderney in the English Channel. The first thing I did on receiving my first pay cheque in Alderney was to set up a joint bank account so that we could start saving towards the row. It was the first step in making the dream a reality and it felt great. We were actually going to do it. Something was happening! The years went by. Ben moved to the Sudan and lived in a container while I moved back to London and became a shipbroker. More years went by. At this stage we were in what could be called the comedy planning phase; for example, we would exchange emails wondering if it was practical to take Ben's Ugandan houseboy, 'Mr Ben', to sea. A sample email from Ben at this time goes: 'Whatever happens . . . death, embarrassment, insanity . . . we must never sink to such lows as wearing Lycra.'

As the years went by we continued to save and to try to agree a date for Ben to come back to the UK so we could prepare for the row. Time passed and other people rowed oceans. One pair who finished the Atlantic in 2006 even had the same names as us. After Ben Fogle and James Cracknell did the Atlantic suddenly everyone knew about ocean rowing. 'Weren't you talking about doing that?' people asked. More time passed and people stopped thinking that we were serious (if they ever had done). I started to become deeply frustrated. Ben moved to Ghana. Still nothing happened, but we continued to say to anyone who would listen that we would definitely do it. People now smiled indulgently in the same way they do if they hear someone is writing a book or becoming an actor.

By the summer of 2009 Ben and I had agreed that he would come back at Christmas with a view to setting off the following June. I needed time to train – time that my hours at HSBC wouldn't allow, so I decided to resign. This might seem strange, but my greatest fear was that it wouldn't happen, that it would simply be another idle dream. I felt that by taking the drastic step of leaving work it would somehow ensure that the row actually happened. My boss, Mark, and the CEO, Chris, were incredibly supportive and said that if I started earlier in the morning I could leave earlier to go to the gym. After all, they said, anything could happen: I could get injured or my friend could pull out. I assured them that the project was one hundred per cent, agreed to stay and started my new training routine the next day. Then in the autumn Ben pulled out. His girlfriend, Carole, had moved out to Africa and he said he couldn't leave her now for what could potentially be ten months at sea. I was devastated. I couldn't accept that the adventure wouldn't happen after years of saving, dreaming and telling everyone I knew about it, including, now, my employers. I understood Ben's reasons, but I felt I would have to go on and do the row somehow, even if it meant going alone, because it had taken on such significance to me over the years.

3 Mixed Motives

> 'When he received the stroke that tore him, he probably felt the agonising bodily laceration, but nothing more. Yet, when by this collision forced to turn towards home, and for long months of days and weeks, Ahab and anguish lay stretched together in one hammock . . . then it was, that his torn body and gashed soul bled into one another.'
>
> Herman Melville, *Moby Dick*

'Why?' is the most frequent question put to the would-be ocean rower. For me, the original inspiration was to have a wild and fun adventure, a sort of glorified fishing trip. Unrealistic perhaps, but this is what sparked my imagination. However, the motivation to actually do it, to actually go through with it despite the obvious risks to life and limb came from something else, something entirely different.

At the age of fourteen I collapsed, breathless, while playing football. Within twenty-four hours I was diagnosed with the rare illness, Guillain-Barre syndrome, rushed to London in an ambulance and hooked up to a life-support machine. When I came round a week later I could not see, breathe, speak, or move a muscle – I was totally paralysed. It was all hugely inconvenient. My immune system had mutinied, mistakenly attacking and destroying the motor nerves, which send messages through the body; although it did the decent thing of leaving the sensory nerves intact so I could feel the pain. There were complications and some close calls, but in the end

I survived. The nerves started regrowing slowly, so that after a month I could breathe and see once more, after four months I could leave hospital in a wheelchair and six months later I was learning to walk again. That might have been the end of that – with six months of pain in Tooting being a good experience for anyone, especially someone who'd grown up in a Home Counties bubble. However, the nerves stopped growing and I was left, still am left I should say, with paralysed feet. The fuckers just don't work. It was a brutal memento, especially during my teenage years when all I really wanted to do was play competitive sport and not have to explain myself every time I met someone new.

Anyway, time passed, as it always does, and to anyone who met me it perhaps seemed like a small thing; to walk with a slight limp is no big deal when compared with the horrors and depredations endured by others around the world. With various foot supports I made wholehearted but usually comedic attempts to play football, hockey, cricket, tennis, squash, to ride horses, scuba dive, hike, ski and all the rest of it. It could be frustrating, but I insisted on pushing myself, on getting a lot out of life. But by my mid-twenties all this effort had buggered my knees, and I was able to do less and less. Simultaneously I found myself becoming more sensitive to innocent comments from people who didn't know me. The reason I took the lift down was to preserve my knees, but their thoughtless comments left me railing: how dare they suggest I was lazy, if only they knew how much effort it takes to walk with paralysed feet. While Tory and I were on a riding safari in Kenya, our guide remarked that, 'James is so lame that if he was a horse he would be put out to pasture.' I was out of earshot at the time but when Tory told me later, I was livid, despite knowing that if I was a horse I would have been shot fourteen years previously. If people wanted to judge me on their own terms, as a totally able-bodied person, then fine, I would do something that most of them would never dare. When I offered to resign in the summer of 2009, my then boss, Mark, asked perceptively if I was doing it to prove a point. He was the first person to ask me this and I'd never thought about it explicitly, but after a second or two I answered, 'Yes', because even then I was completely obsessed about proving that I could do it. It had become a point of pride and there's nothing more dangerous or blind than pride.

4 Monomania

'Considering that with two legs man is but a hobbling wight in all times of danger; considering that the pursuit of whales is always under great and extraordinary difficulties; that every individual moment, indeed, then comprises a peril; under these circumstances is it wise for any maimed man to enter a whale-boat in the hunt?'

Herman Melville, *Moby Dick*

The last word on monomania and obsession goes, of course, to Captain Ahab. He is the central character in Melville's whaling classic, *Moby Dick*. The novel is ostensibly an account of a whaling voyage, although Melville includes many meandering factual deviations on whaling, whales and the sea. Ahab is the captain of the ship and is obsessed with avenging himself on Moby Dick, a white sperm whale that bit off his leg on a previous trip. Ahab ignores the fact that he only has one leg and is unsympathetic to the feelings and lives of others, including his chief mate, Starbuck, who warns him, to no avail, against his headlong pursuit of the white whale. As a model of selfish, relentless focus and unflinching disregard for personal safety, Ahab became a kind of hero to me. It is Ahab's disability which drives him on and I, like the narrator of the book and others before me, was strangely drawn to this. As he says: 'A wild, mystical, sympathetic feeling was in me; Ahab's quenchless feud seemed mine.' Okay, Ahab ends up dead along with all of the crew, bar the narrator, and the white whale survives, but you have to admire the old man's persistence.

With Ben out, I approached a number of friends about doing the row but for one reason or another it wasn't possible or affordable for any of them. I therefore resolved to do it solo. My parents were deeply against the whole idea of me rowing an ocean, convinced that I would die or be seriously injured. I argued that, having felt for so many years like a prisoner inside my own body, it made sense to seek the absolute freedom of being at sea – even if that freedom resulted in death. But these arguments never wash with parents, who have a vested interest in keeping their children alive. With my family against and my friends disinterested the only whole-hearted believer I had at this time was my girlfriend, Tory. Naturally, she was concerned but at the same time she could see how important it was to me. Perhaps, too, she suspected what a nightmare I'd be if I never did the row, and she was right – I would have been.

I knew that it would be very hard to get the project off the ground as an independent solo. The rowing fund had halved since Ben pulled out and the prospect of organising everything by myself, as a first timer, was daunting. I therefore turned to a company called Woodvale Challenge, which organises a race across the Atlantic every two years. They'd put on the races which Cracknell and Fogle and most Atlantic rowers had taken part in. For a fee they would oversee the safety and logistics of the race, offer training support and, vitally, lay on a safety yacht to come and rescue or resupply anyone who got into trouble.

With the Atlantic a well-worn route, I was still keen to do something else, something bigger and wilder – and so they offered this. They were gearing up to run a race across the Indian Ocean in April 2011. They had run an Indian race from

Geraldton in Western Australia to Port Louis, Mauritius in 2009, in which only half the boats had made it. It sounded perfect. The Indian was longer and tougher than the Atlantic and virtually nobody had rowed it. There were around eight teams signed up, a mixture of fours, pairs and solos. I signed up as a solo.

Not long after this, Ben came back on board. An organised event like the Woodvale Indian race meant a safer, shorter trip and he and his girlfriend were keen to move back to the UK. We were back on! We would row an ocean together after all, and while it would be a different ocean than the one we originally planned, it would certainly be as much of an adventure. More people had walked on the moon than had rowed successfully across the Indian Ocean. We would be attempting something not far from unique and, going by the statistics, something very dangerous. But I would be doing it with Ben, as we'd always planned.

5 A Bosom Friend: Ben Stenning

'He seemed to take to me quite as naturally and
unbiddenly as I to him; and when our smoke was
over, he pressed his forehead to mine, clasped me
around the waist, and henceforth we were married;
meaning in his country's phrase, that we were
bosom friends; he would gladly die for me if needs
should be.'

Herman Melville, *Moby Dick*

Ben and I became friends immediately on meeting in the first
week of university. By the end of our first conversation we
were planning a drive from Cairo to Cape Town. By the end
of the first term, when we discovered that we were being two-
timed by the same girl, we were already good enough friends
to laugh the whole thing off.

Ben and I often joked that with our boarding school educa-
tions, gap years and 2:1s from St Andrews, blond hair, blue
eyes and instinctual familiarity with the Home Counties we
were straight off the middle-class conveyor belt. But this was
perhaps unfair as we had both seen a different side of life
even before we pursued our unusual 'career' paths.

After moving to Kenya with his parents, Ben, at the age of
seven, stepped on a stonefish. The year was 1987 and the location was a remote beach near the Tanzanian border. The
stonefish is the most venomous fish in the world and, if
untreated, people often die from the sting. So when Ben limped
along to the local doctor with his mother it was not surprising

that the medical advice was immediate amputation. Ben's mum refused the offer and managed to get him onto a British Airways flight to London the same day. He was admitted to the Centre for Tropical Diseases where they managed to save his life, but complications with the infection meant that he remained there for a further two years while the doctors cut away at the tissue of his foot in an effort to save the limb.

Two years later and with one foot a few sizes smaller than the other, he was discharged and immediately set about taking up as many dangerous pastimes as possible. He later attributed his prodigious sidestep in rugby to having different-sized feet. In 1992, back in Kenya, he captained his school cricket team to the worst defeat in their history in which they managed to post only nine runs in total against Pembroke College, with Ben their top scorer on three.

Then it was back to the UK for secondary school and, after a gap year in Tonga, Ben headed to St Andrews, where we met. What happened over the next four years we would spend many hours trying to piece together while we were at sea; suffice to say we became friends and had lots of fun.

Then Ben moved into a flat in Brixton with me, which is where the dreams of ocean rowing were born. Bizarrely, for an English graduate who wrote his dissertation on post-colonial literature with particular reference to the works of V. S. Naipaul, Ben took a job selling accounting software. His heart wasn't in it and before the year was out he had quit. After a brief stint working at the World Cheese Awards he went back to Africa and took a job in logistics.

Initially he was based in Uganda, where his recklessness was able to flourish with regular white-water rafting trips and frequent forays into the war-torn north. On one occasion he was imprisoned in the Congo on suspicion of spying, but managed to bribe his way out. Growing bored with Uganda, he got a posting to the Sudan where he lived in a container and had further accident-prone adventures, including having to be airlifted out with the dual afflictions of amoebic dysentery and Nairobi eye. My favourite of his misadventures was the time one of the company's trucks broke down in a massive swamp the size of Belgium called the Sudd. Unable to bear the heat in the front cabin, Ben and the Indian driver were forced out onto the uncovered carriage. However, the mosquitoes were so thick that they blotted out the moon and the stars and they were soon feasting on Ben and the driver. Cursing his penchant for short shorts and sleeveless shirts he formulated a plan with his colleague. They decided to strip naked and cover themselves in diesel. They spent the rest of the night smoking and exchanging life stories in the nude.

After Sudan, Ben moved to Ghana, which was more civilised if less interesting. Three years later, Ben handed in his notice and came back to the UK to prepare for the row.

I never formally assessed Ben as a potential partner in our rowing enterprise. He'd always been my friend and we'd always planned to do it together as mates. Of course he was accident prone, reckless and had no sea experience whatsoever, but then I had exactly the same credentials. Both as bad as each other, we always seemed to compound the trouble that one or the other got into. But being as bad as each other can be an advantage – it assures parity. Also, these seeming negatives were far outweighed by Ben's many qualities: his great sense of humour, his impulsive generosity, his polymath interests. Spending months at sea with a friend who didn't take himself too seriously was far more important than setting off with someone who had all the right qualifications . . . even if the friend in question was insisting on bringing a pair of salmon pink short shorts.

6 Preparations

'Why did I do it? Because at the end of my days,
I'm going to be lying in my bed looking at my toes,
and I'm going to ask my toes questions like "Have
I really enjoyed life? Have I done everything I've
wanted to do?" And if the answer is no, I'm going
to be really pissed off.'

Chay Blyth

One summer's evening at Gallions Reach Marina in east
London we inspected a second hand boat which had crossed
the Atlantic twice. Despite being a sturdy twenty-three-foot
boat she looked impossibly small and slightly surreal sat, as
she was, on a rusty old trailer in this forgotten part of London.
Sitting on the sliding rowing seat, gazing at the glistening
towers of Canary Wharf to the west, I found it hard to imagine
what life at sea on her might be like. But we needed a boat
and she was cheap and according to the owners she floated.
We provisionally named her *Brixton Dreamer* and set about
planning many modifications.

A friend, Christian, with an upmarket web design company
called Marmalade on Toast, drunkenly agreed to do our
website in the early hours at a wedding and so we were the
proud owners of a swish new site. We chose charities to raise
money for. Ben picked a Kenyan orphanage, Tumani Homes,
while I went with the GBS Support Group. Training at the
gym had begun in earnest and we were both getting stronger,

building up to either a two-hour row on the machine or a two-hour swim in the pool six days a week. We agreed with my friend Adam, a producer, to make a film about the trip and started filming our training and preparations. We also managed to get a title sponsor, Baxter Healthcare UK, which gave our dwindling bank account a much-needed boost. They also ran a competition for naming our boat with the winner choosing *Indian Runner*, after the flightless ducks. Everything was looking good.

Then, around this time, I met up with two people planning on rowing the Indian in the same race as us. Ollie Wells was part of the four-man campaign aiming to break the four's record and Rob Eustace was a solo who had rowed the Atlantic with Woodvale in 2007 as a pair. They had bad news. There were questions over Woodvale, and in particular over the feasibility of the 2011 Indian race. Rob said he had decided to do the race as an independent and he didn't think any of the teams listed on Woodvale's website would do it, apart from us. Ollie had read that Woodvale's boss, a serial ocean rower named Simon Chalk, had been declared bankrupt. We had unthinkingly been paying our hard-saved money to Woodvale in instalments and had never questioned their viability as a company. I immediately emailed Simon to ask him how many people were taking part and if the race was definitely going ahead. Up until this point he had been quite elusive but he gave a long reply outlining the situation in response to my email. The only two teams definitely in the race were the four and ourselves. The event could go ahead, he said, but it wasn't workable to have a support yacht. For a reduced fee Woodvale would still run an unsupported row. We were guaranteed a podium place, as long as we could finish. We agreed immediately, while the four-man team called a meeting with Simon and their families to discuss the proposal.

The meeting was held the day after the Four's fundraising ball. It was a glittering affair in the Hurlingham Club. Everyone seemed to be there: friends of mine, ocean rowers, even the guys who'd sold us our boat. I called Ben in Africa halfway through the party to say that we needed to do more to promote ourselves. 'Friends keep asking me why I'm here. I don't think anyone has any idea we're the only other team rowing across the Indian Ocean next year,' I said. In the end we never did very well on that front. Anyway, I went to the meeting the next day with Tory and there we met Simon. He was shorter and fatter than you might imagine for someone who had rowed across four oceans, including the Indian, solo. But he was clearly experienced and had a softly spoken affability and calmness. He was a fascinating character. Every time one of the Four's parents expressed a concern about the lack of a safety yacht, the organisation of the row or his finances Simon would allay it with calm confidence. But then, as they were nodding in relieved understanding, he'd follow up these reassurances with a story about a shark which followed him on the Indian for 50 days, or about the time he capsized during his 2002 attempt and had to sit on the upturned hull for a night while awaiting rescue. He'd then sit back with a mischievous grin, revelling in the new uncertainty, and wait for the next question. He advised everyone to not bother with the gym but to make sure instead that our boats were ready. He gave the impression that everything was under control for our Indian row and, after all the knowledge he'd shared, I was as sold as the Four, who now also agreed to go it alone without the safety yacht. I even phoned Ben again in Africa to say something along the lines of, 'Don't worry, we're in good hands.'

* * *

We met Simon one more time in the UK, before leaving for Australia. Ben was back in December for our navigation course and we'd arranged for Simon to come and have a look at our boat. He turned up six hours late but stayed into the early hours. He gave us a slightly veiled piece of advice along the lines of, 'Get cracking, you won't have any help.' We didn't think to ask more, but then a week or so later we discovered online that Simon was about to set off and lead a crew of twelve pay-per-place rowers across the Atlantic. It would be his fifth ocean row. The secretary at Woodvale told us that Simon would see us in Australia three weeks before we set off for the safety checks and that was that. We'd signed up to Woodvale because of the promise of the safety net and logistical help, but we now found there was no support boat and that we were organising everything, such as the shipping, ourselves. We had arrived back at the independent row we were originally planning on, only with less money.

Ben came back to England for good in January 2011 and, having finished our jobs, we started a manic month's work on the boat. We were storing the boat on a farm in Winchester, where a boat builder called Neil was constructing a forty-foot yacht. He had tools and experience. Patiently he explained the difference between bolts and screws and showed us how to do one thing or another before deciding that it would be quicker to do it himself. We must have bamboozled him somewhat; two massively impractical, office-working humanities graduates about to set off across the Indian Ocean with no relevant experience whatsoever. Still, we managed to get the boat finished in time to load it into a container in Southampton at the start of February, and booked our flights to Australia to coincide with her arrival in Fremantle. We would ship her across the Indian Ocean in a container and then row her straight back.

With the boat gone, we reverted to the more familiar territory of shopping and drinking. Sitting in the pub we'd enthuse about the voyage and agree that we were just aiming to make it across and have a great experience rather than break any records. The shopping was a necessary evil. One trip that stands out was a visit to Boots. We had been told by a watermaker expert to buy some condoms to cover a part of our desalinator. We decided to buy them in Boots along with some other essentials. We got to the checkout with ten bottles of sun cream, two tubs of Vaseline and a packet of condoms. The checkout girl looked at our basket and then at us and said, 'Going on holiday?' When we explained that we were going to sea together she seemed to understand.

I was quite stressed during this period: making lists, worrying, planning. Ben was a lot more relaxed about everything and always insisted on taking his afternoon siesta. This could be a comfort but aware that Ben knew as little as I did about boats and navigation it was also slightly concerning.

In March we had our leaving party. I was touched by the presence of our friends and family, who were there to help us fulfil our dream. Although, in among the games, which included Indian leg wrestling, I still managed to worry. In short, I was afraid of failure. All of our friends had sponsored us, had come to our party and it would be a disaster, I thought, if we were to only last a few days at sea for whatever reason. Having spent months planning and nearly every last penny on getting the boat out to Australia the idea of failure terrified me.

It was clear to me then that I had learnt, no doubt at school, one of life's worst pieces of habitual thought, namely that effort is vulgar and that it's better to make a mockery of something than to be seen to try and fail. I knew I would have to unpick this psychological knot eventually, but in the meantime I commanded myself to not bore anyone else with these worries.

7 'Leaving on a Jet Plane'

> 'Far better it is to dare mighty things, to win glorious
> triumphs even though chequered by failure, than to
> rank with those poor spirits who neither enjoy nor
> suffer much because they live in the gray twilight
> that knows neither victory nor defeat.'
> Theodore Roosevelt, 'The Strenuous Life'

My sister and her husband drove us to Heathrow on a cold
March night. Saying goodbye to Tory was hard, especially with
my brother-in-law filming us, but we had talked everything
through and she'd selflessly told me to go, enjoy the adventure
and not to think too much about home.

'One last thing, if you're ever in a dangerous situation in
which you really have to fight to stay alive, promise me that
you will, that you'll never give up.'

'I promise. Everything will be fine. I'm very hard to kill,' I
said, trying to make light of her fears.

For as long as we'd been together I'd talked about the
rowing, so none of this was a surprise to her; she'd been a
massive help at every step of the way. For years she'd enthused
about the rowing and shared in the dream, and in a hundred
practical ways she'd helped us, from painting the boat to
helping us pack the food into the holds. I felt bad to be leaving
her for so many months and no matter how much I played
it down I knew there was a risk. I thought about Tory all the
way to Dubai, but by the time we were flying down to Perth

I was caught up in the excitement of it all again and intent on following her advice to enjoy the experience.

'Where are you boys off to then?' asked the customs official in Perth, eyeing our team jackets. We had a couple of very fancy sailing jackets sponsored by Quba Sails, which made us look a lot more professional than we really were.

'We're going to row from Geraldton to Mauritius,' I said.

'What, out there on the ogin?' he said, shaking his head in disbelief. 'Good on ya.'

We got the same reaction from most of the Aussies we met. We were just another couple of mad Poms heading out into the ogin, never to be seen again. We stayed in Perth for a week with friends of Ben's. Perth got its name as the 'City of Light' when, on 20 February 1962, residents all turned on their houselights, car lights, street lights and any other lights they could lay their hands on so that American astronaut John Glenn would be able to see the city when he passed over during his orbit of the earth on *Friendship 7*. They repeated this treat for Glenn when he passed overhead again in 1998 on the *Discovery*, when he became the oldest man to go into space at the age of 77.

During our time in Perth we cleared our boat through customs with the help of an agent, the unfortunately named but highly efficient Peter Sutcliffe. We then got a lift 400 kilometres up the west coast with family friends who lived in Geraldton, our starting point. As we sped through the Australian outback, dodging kangaroos in the dying light, it was hard to imagine exactly what it would be like putting to sea in our little boat. The ocean off Perth had seemed so serene. But it would surely be rough; the statistics for ocean rowing boats spoke for themselves.

8 A Brief Note on the Indian Ocean Rowing Statistics

'The Indian Ocean, the most savage of the three.'
Bernard Moitessier, *The Long Way*

When we set off in April 2011 the statistics for rowing a boat from Australia across the Indian Ocean did not help calm our nerves. The success rate was low and the stories that accompanied each failure were frightening.

Only eight pairs had ever attempted the Indian, of which only two had made it across. Those two pairs both did so in the 2009 Woodvale race, with a support yacht following them. The six pairs who didn't make it were spread out from 2002 to 2009. Looking at the stats we had to ask ourselves, was it just that the 2009 pairs got lucky? A 25 per cent success rate was troubling indeed, especially given that 18 of the 20 pairs who started Woodvale's 2009 Atlantic race finished.

The two pairs who finished the Indian did it in 102 and 103 days respectively. There were diverse reasons for the other pairs not finishing. In 2002 Simon Chalk and a friend attempted to be the first pair to cross but, according to Simon, they were holed by either a stray container or the periscope of a submarine. They had to cling to the upturned hull all night until they were rescued the following day. Another British pair was rescued after a storm battered them for 72 hours, resulting in injury and broken equipment. They had been at sea for 46 days. A Russian pair managed 24 days before their watermaker broke. Roger Haines, who gave us lots of help before we left, and his fellow rower had to abandon their attempt when Roger broke a vertebra just one day in (he went on to complete the Atlantic solo after recovering from injury, crossing in 93 days in 2010). The same year another pair called a halt when steering problems prevented them getting off the shelf after an 11-day battle.

The solos had a 50 per cent success rate, with three managing to cross from six attempts, while the bigger crews of four or more fared better, with four crossings and one failure.

SOLOS

Name	From	To	Depart	Arrival	Days
Simon Chalk	Kalbarri, Western Australia	Longitude of Rafael Island	February 27, 2003	June 15, 2003	107
Sarah Outen	Fremantle, Western Australia	Mauritius	April 1, 2009	August 3, 2009	124
Erden Eruc	Carnarvon, Western Australia	Mahajanga, Madagascar	July 13, 2010	November 26, 2010	136

[3 failures]

PAIRS

Name	From	To	Depart	Arrival	Days
Andrew Delaney & Guy Watts	Geraldton, Western Australia	Port Louis, Mauritius	April 19, 2009	July 30, 2009	102

| James Thysse & James Facer-Childs | Geraldton, Western Australia | Port Louis, Mauritius | April 19, 2009 | July 31, 2009 | 103 |

[6 failures]

FOURS

Name	From	To	Depart	Arrival	Days
Phil McCorry, Nick McCorry, Matt Hellier & Ian Allen	Geraldton, Western Australia	Port Louis, Mauritius	April 19, 2009	June 26, 2009	68
Sarah Duff, Fiona Waller, Jo Jackson & Elin Haf Davis	Geraldton, Western Australia	Port Louis, Mauritius	April 19, 2009	July 6, 2009	78
Tom Wigram, Billy Gammon, Mat Hampel & Pete Staples	Geraldton, Western Australia	Port Louis, Mauritius	April 19, 2009	July 9, 2009	81

[1 failure]

source: www.oceanrowing.com

These statistics were sobering, especially when compared to those for the Atlantic. Of the 169 pairs to attempt the mid-Atlantic route over the years, 145 have been successful with only 24 coming a cropper. Apart from being 600 miles shorter than the Indian crossing, the Canaries to Caribbean row is blessed by more dependable trade winds and generally more favourable currents. When rowers leave from the Canary Islands they are in deep water straight away and don't have to contend with the shallow continental shelf which stretches away from Western Australia for hundreds of miles. Looking at the statistics before we left we could see that all the pairs had either been rescued or had spent over a hundred days at sea. Whatever happened to us we could see that there would be drama. It was finally happening.

9 The Shortest Possible Description of the Lead-up to Our Departure, Including a Brief Portrait of the Incomparable Simon Chalk

'Good humoured, easy and careless, he presided over
his whale-boat as if the deadliest encounters were
but a dinner, and his crew all invited guests.'
Herman Melville, *Moby Dick*

We waited in Geraldton for Simon Chalk and our boat, two
fairly important parts of our row, which were supposedly
coming together. The four-man team was all the while deeply
concerned about Woodvale and Simon. He had built their
boat and they needed various bits of equipment from him.
They were getting quite stressed about the situation having
set out very publicly, with some high-profile sponsors like
B&Q, to beat the Indian Ocean four's record of 68 days.
The days went by without Simon or the boat arriving. It felt
like everything was descending into farce.

In the end Simon turned up – with his impish grin and
full of bold stories and jovial advice – but without the boats.
The next day we bumped into the four-man crew on the beach
and they had bad news. Simon had disappeared again. He had
driven down to Perth and, just before boarding a plane, had
sent them an email explaining how he had to fly to Barbados
to meet a pair who were finishing the Atlantic.

We now started to realise that we were completely on our own and might have to set off by ourselves without any shore support. We decided to stop speaking to anyone back in the UK because we were finding it difficult to lie and say everything was going fine. We paid to have the boats hauled up to Geraldton from Fremantle and started on our last-minute preparations.

At this point Rob Eustace, the independent solo, turned up with his boat. Tony Humphreys, his weather router and safety officer, was with him. He had been the safety officer on Woodvale's big Atlantic races in the past, but had fallen out with Simon and left. Unless you asked Simon, in which case he'd been sacked for incompetence. Ocean rowing, we were discovering, was a small world with plenty of politics and clashing personalities.

In the end Simon turned up in Geraldton again. Having initially tiptoed around each other like spurned lovers, Simon and Tony were soon getting on famously and, burying the hatchet, they quickly came to an arrangement that Tony would be our safety officer. In payment, Simon would apparently give him some old boat he had back in the UK. By then this sort of carry-on seemed almost normal, so we all agreed. Still, Simon knocked around in Australia until we left, helping out, drinking whisky on our boat with us and mouthing the answers to key safety questions behind Tony's back so that we could pass the final sign-off.

Simon did give us some good advice. 'Stay positive, take care of each other and enjoy it' was his philosophy in a nutshell. He also fervently believed that, apart from serious injury, the only reason people stopped rowing was because they had given up psychologically. Broken kit, minor ailments, leaks – these were all excuses. There was a way of getting around every problem, he argued, and stubbornness would always prevail.

This approach made us even more determined not to quit for any reason, no matter the danger. Our mindset would get us through.

Simon dominated our conversations when he wasn't there, too. He seemed to us essentially like a modern-day corsair: affable, charming, amusing, interesting and relentlessly positive, but a pirate nonetheless. If you were on a rowing boat with him you'd never run out of conversation and you could absolutely trust him with your life but, as with any pirate, you wouldn't leave him in charge of your accounts or your harem. We liked him.

10 Australia

'Having little or no money in my purse, and nothing particular to interest me on shore, I thought I would sail about a little and see the watery part of the world.'

Herman Melville, *Moby Dick*

All the shenanigans that led to Tony becoming our safety officer didn't help instil confidence, although we remained outwardly gung-ho. The main problem was that neither Ben nor I really knew what we were doing. This manifested itself in different ways. Ben would act quickly and without thinking, so I would come back and find him drilling random holes or sticking things on the boat without any real idea of what he was trying to achieve. I, on the other hand, would act painfully slowly, insisting on discussing, analysing and agreeing every move. Despite these differences, we always got on very well and were able to laugh about everything in the end.

As we got closer to our departure date, Ben was impatient to be gone while I was still dithering, saying we needed more time to get this, that or the other. Most of it probably wasn't important, but I still maintain we should have taken toilet paper, which Ben insisted wasn't important. He thought we could use the wet wipes we had on board, which were actually intended to remove the salt from our bodies. I wasn't happy and said he'd have to come up with an alternative if we ran out, even if it meant cutting his clothing into strips. This was fine by him as long as we could get the hell out of Geraldton as soon as possible. We were both bored of the small town and had run out of money.

Added motivation to leave Geraldton came one morning when on the way to the hardware store in our hire car I answered my mobile and immediately saw flashing blue lights. I pulled over on the quiet street.

'Do you know why I've pulled you over, mate?' scolded the policeman.

'Oh dear, don't tell me it's against the law here to talk on a mobile phone while driving?'

'Too right it is and it's a fifty dollar fine. Can I see your licence?'

'Absolutely, officer.'

'This licence expired three months ago. You need a new one and a new photo, mate; you don't look like that any more.'

'I honestly had no idea about the licence and I'm still coming to terms with the face.'

'Well, I'm afraid driving without a licence is a court summons. When and how are you planning to leave Australia?'

'On Friday, by ocean rowing boat.'

'Oh Jeez, you're one of these bloody Poms from down the yacht club. Well, it's your responsibility to pay the fine and arrange a court hearing before you leave.'

Contrary to what everyone says maybe you *can* over-prepare for an ocean row. So Ben and I agreed to head off on the Thursday.

When we finally put the boat in the water she sat very low with the weight of 120 days' worth of provisions. Worryingly, water flooded onto the deck through the scuppers. Was this normal? We had no idea; we'd never rowed her before. Our first row, around to the marina, was a disaster. We put the oars in the rowlocks the wrong way round, as someone kindly pointed out to us, and then we nearly washed onto some rocks because we couldn't work out how to use the foot-steering system.

Another concern was our watermaker. Powered by solar panels, the watermaker is key to the success of any ocean row as it is impossible to carry enough fresh water for the crew. We had an old model, mounted somewhat incorrectly, but we had got it serviced in England and Simon said he thought it looked okay. Tony showed us how to repressurise it if we ran into trouble and we then trialled it in the marina. A slow trickle of fresh water came out. In an hour we made five litres. We were overjoyed that it worked.

'How many litres did you make?' asked James Kayll, the captain of the four-man team, who had sauntered down the pontoon to where we were tied up.

'Five litres!' replied Ben excitedly.

'Oh, we've just made five litres in ten minutes with our one.'

Ben and I exchanged a look. It never does to compare yourself to other people in life. We had water and five litres an hour would be enough for us, as long as the watermaker held up. Anyway, if the electric one failed we had a backup hand pump and, regardless of how hard people said it was to pump for two hours a day, we were determined to use it to get across if we had to.

A few days before we were due to leave we went to wave Rob off in his solo boat. It was strange to see him heading out into the ocean. We watched as he diminished into a tiny speck on the horizon and then we turned back to our preparations. Two days later he was back. He had got bad food poisoning and some issues on the home front had come up. He wouldn't be going back out again. He was fit, highly organised and had previously rowed the Atlantic, so this development further heightened our anxiety. As did his comment in the pub: 'I don't want to scare you guys but very soon someone will die rowing an ocean.' This didn't scare us; it terrified us. If anyone was going to die it would surely be us, complete novices who had only practised for a grand total of three hours.

What's more, we knew we would have a baptism of fire on 'the shelf'.

11 The Shelf

> 'Now then, I thought, unconsciously rolling up the
> sleeves of my frock, here goes for a cool, collected
> dive at death and destruction, and the devil fetch
> the hindmost.'
>
> Herman Melville, *Moby Dick*

Western Australia is seen by most seafarers as the hardest coast
to get away from in a rowing boat. This is one of the main
reasons why the Indian Ocean is so much harder to row across
than the Atlantic. A quick glance at a navigational chart shows
a large continental shelf off the west coast of Australia that
extends hundreds of miles into the ocean. It ends quite
abruptly and the depth of the sea above it goes from 50 metres
to 5,000 metres in no time at all. The shallowness created by
the shelf creates very short, sharp seas. Swells travel over
thousands of miles of open ocean and don't break until they
hit the shelf, which means big waves.

Conditions are made worse by the wind. As the Australian
desert heats during the day the air expands and travels out to
sea where it cools and creates an on-shore breeze. So every
night the winds conspire to blow you back towards the
Australian coast. Thus, this localised weather tries to suck you
back towards land each night over the choppy seas of the
shelf.

In the 2009 Indian race, two pairs, one solo and one four-man
team all fell victim to the shelf. The teams who managed to

get out to deep water had to spend the first ten days battling to reach it.

We knew all this about the winds, the currents, the depth of the sea; we had met Roger Haines, who had to stop in 2009 after breaking one of his vertebrae on the shelf after being thrown off his rowing seat by a wave. We had heard other stories, too, and they all contributed to our fear.

What had started off all those years ago as a vague dream was now about to become a reality. What exact reality we were letting ourselves in for, though, we had little idea.

PART TWO

All at Sea

12 The First Day

'After all the years of training, now there is reality,
a chance to be fulfilled and make one joyous leap
clear of time and the pettiness of life.'
John Ridgeway (on starting his row
across the North Atlantic)

We set off at dawn on Thursday 21 April. It was a calm morning
and as the amber glow of sunrise started to light up the quiet
little marina we untied and pushed off.

We'd had a quick look at the weather on Tony's computer.
The plan we'd agreed was a vague one: head fifty miles north-
west to a small group of islands called the Abrolhos and, after
clearing the northernmost island, push west into deeper water.
After that we were to row west while trying not to be pushed
too far north too quickly by the prevailing weather, which
tends to come from the south in the Indian Ocean. A quick
round of handshakes with Simon and the four-man team and
we were off.

'The clock's ticking,' joked Tony as we pushed off and took
our first few strokes.

As we slowly made our way out of the marina I tried to
ignore the butterflies in my stomach. This is what you wanted,
I said to myself, this is what you asked for and now it's
happening.

We left rowing together, Ben in the bow position on the
foot steering, while I sat in front. Every so often I got up and

changed the position of our small film camera, moving the shot from us to the shoreline where the giant grain silos of the port were now illuminated in the golden light of dawn.

It took what felt like an inordinate amount of time to row out of the marina.

'Come on, mate, row a bit harder; this is embarrassing.'

'Do you want to do some rowing as well?'

'I can't, I'm steering.'

'Can't you do both at once?'

'Actually, it's quite hard.'

'Careful of that yacht.'

'Shhh, let's stop arguing; the others are watching.'

We eventually made it out, but it felt peculiar to row out of the marina and into open water, knowing that we were about to spend months at sea. It felt like psyching yourself up to do a bungee jump: you know there's a safety rope attached to you but it's against basic human nature to jump off a bridge. After all the years of saving and all the long months of preparation here we were, heading out to sea.

Warren, a family friend based in Geraldton, and his daughter had come to see us off on a jet ski. They circled us for twenty minutes or so as we navigated our way slowly out of Geraldton. Before they left Warren threw a toy kangaroo into the boat, a present for a friend of his in Mauritius, and then with a loud rev of the engine they were gone. As the noise of the jet ski dwindled, our new world seemed suddenly quiet. Nothing but the tap-lap of the water on the side of the boat and the creaking dip of the oars.

'I can't believe we're actually doing this,' I said.

'Woohoo!' screamed Ben at the top of his voice.

'Whatever happens we can't turn back.'

'Definitely. There's no way we're going back to Geraldton.'

We had entered a number of waypoints into our GPS to

help see us through the queues of cargo ships waiting to load grain or iron ore at the port. The steel ships loomed large as we neared but we cruised safely past them at a nice rate of about two knots. *This is easy*, I thought. Apart from the fact that rowing together was proving a bit awkward as we kept clashing oars.

'Mate, you're rowing way too fast – we've got over three thousand miles to go,' I said.

'Come on, Adair, stop fannying about with the camera and concentrate on the rowing.'

'I still can't believe we're actually doing this.'

'Woohoo!'

During the first morning the swell was around two metres and we shouted excitedly as we ran briefly down the waves. We recorded a top speed of 6.2 knots on one wave. Things were going well, better than expected. We cleared the outer limits of the port and started to head for the aptly named North Island, the northernmost isle of the Abrolhos group. We rowed the first six hours together and then I, having lost a bet, had to row the first shift alone.

The rowing was fine; I didn't feel tired but I did start to feel queasy. By the end of my two-hour shift I felt positively sick. A two-hour lie-down didn't help. When I came out for my next shift at dusk I sat down on the rowing seat and promptly threw up over the side. Luckily, following Simon's advice, I had only eaten tinned fruit that day so it came up very easily.

'Are you okay?' asked Ben.

'Yeah, fine,' I said, leaning over the side again to throw up.

As we entered our first night I felt better with an empty stomach. I clipped myself onto the boat with the sort of cord that surfers use. It was disorientating being on such a small boat, unable to see where the waves were coming from. The lights of the coast were clearly visible, but as the daylight faded I was treated to the most amazing sight: more stars than I'd ever seen before. It was incredible. Every few minutes a shooting star would streak across the sky. Beneath us the bioluminescence lit up green and gold whenever the oars broke the water. This was the wild beauty we'd dreamt of. But, as night wore on, the on-shore breeze picked up and throughout the night we took it in turns to row into it, trying with all our might simply to stay stationary.

13 At the Mercy of the Shelf

'The oarsmen violently forced their boat through
the sledge-hammering seas.'
Herman Melville, *Moby Dick*

Daybreak on our second day didn't herald much of a respite.
The wind stayed against us. We were exhausted after our first
night on the ocean and we didn't yet have our sea legs, which
meant we were crawling around our tiny boat like a couple of
drunks. I couldn't stomach any of our freeze-dried food or snacks
so, apart from a tin of fruit, I ate nothing. We tried to row into
the wind but by mid-morning we decided it was pointless and
we'd be best to deploy the parachute anchor, which inflates
underwater and limits the travel of the boat backwards.

The only small issue was that we'd never deployed one
before and had only had a half-hour briefing from Simon and
Tony back in Geraldton, a town we were going to see again
sooner than we might have hoped if the wind kept blowing
us backwards. Ben got the para anchor out and then paused.

'Which end are we supposed to tie it to again?'

'I'm pretty sure it's the bow. I guess it's the bow we want
pointing into the wind.'

'Can we stop using nautical terms, it's confusing. Front or
back?'

'Ben, it's a boat, I think we should use nautical terms.'

'But you only learnt the difference between bow and the
other one a couple of days ago.'

'Stern.'

'Back.'

'Whatever; let's put this thing on one end and see if it works.'

'Okay, I'm pretty sure it was actually the back; that means the biggest surface area against which the wind can push to inflate the parachute.'

'That makes sense, right let's deploy it off the stern.'

'Agreed, let's put it off the back.'

We then debated some more about which rope attached to what and where the retrieval line should be tied. Ben admitted he'd forgotten how to tie a bowline knot, so I did the knots while he paid out the line.

The para anchor was in and it made an immediate difference. We stayed on it until late afternoon, lying in the cabin, regaining our strength. We would need it that night. Having pulled in the para anchor we set off again, rowing in two-hour shifts, trying to get away from the coast. Throughout the night we fought the on-shore breeze and managed to stay pretty much where we were. By daybreak on Day 3 we were a total of thirty-one miles from Geraldton with about twenty miles left until North Island.

Our third day at sea was beautiful. The sun shone hard and wildlife swarmed around us. Gulls and petrels flew overhead while jellyfish and seaweed drifted below. However, we were still in sight of land and the occasional butterflies that fluttered around the boat reminded us how close we remained. Despite our excitement and the hot sun we'd promised ourselves not to swim, play music or relax at all until we were off the shelf, so we did nothing but row and sleep in those first days. By now the seasickness had worn off and we were tentatively trying our first freeze-dried meals. After a few mouthfuls we'd throw the rest overboard and declare another variety of meal completely inedible. The only one we could finish for the first week or so was porridge.

As the sun went down on Day 3 we were presented with our biggest test yet: the relentless on-shore wind pushing us back to Australia. We rowed flat out for twelve hours into this headwind. Every time we tried to point the bow into the wind it would push us around so that we were beam on. In some ways it was better than being on the para anchor because at least we were doing something, battling the wind instead of just lying in the cabin while drifting slowly backwards. But mentally it was very draining having to row with one oar for so much of the time as we tried to bring the boat round to point in the right direction. However, we were absolutely determined to get off the shelf and we had convinced ourselves before setting off that it would be the toughest part of the trip, so we fought hard and proudly reported to each other at the end of each shift how little distance we'd been pushed backwards. By the end of the night we'd limited our travel back to Australia to a mere two nautical miles, a relative triumph.

'It's now clear why the Indian is so tough,' I wrote shakily in my journal.

14 Downing Tools

'There are certain queer times and occasions in this strange mixed affair we call life when a man takes this whole Universe for a vast practical joke.'

Herman Melville, *Moby Dick*

By the time the sun came up on Day 4 we were in serious pain. Our hands and bottoms ached as they tried to adjust to their new workload of twelve hours a day. My fingers were in particular agony while Ben was finding it hard to sit down. We found that even while we weren't rowing our hands remained locked in position as if we were gripping imaginary oars. We called this affliction 'claw hand' and it would dog us for many weeks to come.

'Claw hand' did some damage to our campaign on Day 4. As we had rowed hard through the previous night, fighting against the elements, the rowlocks on our boat kept coming loose. At this stage it was a two-man job to fix them, with one person locking the bolt at the bottom tight while the other turned the nut on the top to tighten the rowlock again. There we were, Ben leaning over the side with our most important tool, the brand-new pair of dolphin nose pliers, while I was balancing on the gunwale with the second most important tool, the only spanner that fitted these nuts perfectly. 'Ready,' said Ben, who had his hand over the side locking the bolt in place. I started to turn the screw and then all of a sudden my claw hand seized and I dropped the spanner overboard. Seeing the spanner sinking, Ben reached down and tried to grab it and in doing so managed to drop the pliers. We watched as the stainless steel tools disappeared soundlessly into the blue. We then looked at each other and burst out laughing. What else could we do, losing two of our most important tools so early on like that.

'At least we've still got Paddington,' I joked. Ben had lashed a small Paddington Bear, a gift from his mum, to the prow the day before we left.

'And the solar-powered fairy lights,' he replied, referring to a gift from my sister.

'We've definitely got our priorities right.'

In the end we managed to find an adjustable spanner and, in conjunction with a one-size-too-big spanner held at an angle, we fixed the rowlock. It wouldn't be the last time we would have to do running repairs with odd-fitting tools.

Later in the day the wind changed to come from behind us and we used the respite to row like maniacs for North Island. It seemed easy to get through the pain and discomfort we felt in those early days because we were so intent on getting off the shelf. Our energy levels and enthusiasm were still high. By the dawn of Day 5 we were nearing our waypoint at the northern tip of the Abrolhos.

The Abrolhos was the scene of an infamous shipwreck and mutiny when the *Batavia*, a Dutch East India Company vessel, ran aground on 4 June 1629. The ship had been deliberately steered off course when a bankrupted pharmacist, Jeronimus Cornelisz, conceived of a plan to start a new life in some distant land and to bankroll it with the trading gold on board. Cornelisz had been fleeing religious persecution in Holland but when the vessel was wrecked he turned persecutor enlisting the help of the other mutineers to enact the cold-blooded slaughter of over one hundred of the survivors during the following months. Justice, or revenge, was eventually done when escaped members of the crew, including the captain, returned to the islands with reinforcements from the Dutch trading post at Batavia, modern day Jakarta. Their 33-day trip there in an open boat is a story in itself and is famous as an early feat in navigation and courage. On their return most of the mutineers were executed, Cornelisz's second in command was broken on the wheel whilst Cornelisz had his hands hacked off before being hanged. Two of the lesser mutineers were marooned on the mainland where their genetic legacy has been traced among the Aboriginal people who must have adopted them. The episode endured as a lesson that even the supposedly civilised Europeans could be reduced to shocking barbarities when they considered themselves beyond the reach of the law and consequently the punishments for mutiny remained remorseless amongst the great seafaring nations.

Knowing of this dark episode in the history of the islands added to the treacherous atmosphere of the shelf. The bare islands we had to row past were proven ship wreckers, the conditions infamously difficult and we felt as far away from home as those who had shipped aboard the *Batavia* some three hundred and eighty years before us must have felt.

'We're eight miles from North Island and the end of the shelf,' I wrote in my journal, but I was wrong; the shelf was by no means finished with us yet.

15 The Looming Seas

'The vast swells of the omnipotent sea.'
Herman Melville, *Moby Dick*

With the wind behind us, we made North Island in quick time so that we could stop in sight of the infamous breaking wave that crashes over the island's north-westerly tip. After carrying out some repairs, including the troublesome rowlocks, we had our lunch and, given the heat, started debating the merits of having our first swim. It seemed appropriate given the calm conditions and the fact that we'd managed to reach what we thought was the edge of the shelf. Then, just as we were agreeing that a swim would be nice, a massive shark breached the ocean about twenty metres away. The shark's jaws snapped shut as it crashed back down, taking with it a sea bird that had been floating along on the surface.

'I think that was a great white,' I shouted excitedly.

'Definitely, that was massive.'

'Shall we put off the swim for a bit?'

'Definitely.'

Now we had reached North Island we turned west and started to head directly out into the Indian Ocean. As we rowed west we were unnerved by the looming swell. The sea appeared completely calm but the glassy surface rolled in massive, undulating waves. At first we thought they would surely break on us and we held onto the sides of the boat in fear and anticipation. Instead they picked us up and put us down without a drop of water getting in the boat or a ripple breaking the surface. All the while, the blue sky and occasional clouds were reflected in these strange seas. We called this place 'the looming sea' and it seemed to herald the start of our adventures in deep water. *Will it be like this all the way?* we wondered naively.

As we rowed out to sea more fins appeared behind us. I stopped rowing and fumbled with our film camera but I was too slow, they disappeared beneath us. Not long after this a huge pod of dolphins swam past us. Scores of them were breaching and jumping all around us.

As the sun started to go down the vermillion sky was reflected eerily in the silent, looming swells. Stars started to emerge and, after the nights battling away into headwinds, everything seemed charmed and easy. Throughout the night we took it in turns as before, but with one slightly longer shift to give the other person a bit more sleep. And so the four-hour night shift was born. At the beginning of my longer sleep I lay awake for a few minutes with the hatch above my head open. The stars swam in front of my eyes as the looming seas lifted and lowered us gently so that it felt as if we were a ship adrift in space.

When I took over from Ben later in the night he reported seeing whales right next to the boat, slapping their tails on the surface. In my long night shift I listened out but heard nothing. As we edged ever further out to sea the sweeping light of North Island's lighthouse got fainter and fainter until it was swallowed up by the night. We had lost sight of land.

16 The Vortex

'The wildest winds of heaven and earth conspire to
cast her on the treacherous, slavish shore.'
Herman Melville, *Moby Dick*

By lunch on Day 6 the wind was starting to pick up and
consequently the seas became choppy and uneven. A large
cargo ship appeared about two miles from us and I tried to
speak to the master on our VHF radio. He didn't hear or
wouldn't answer and kept ploughing on. As the afternoon
wore on the wind built against us, pushing us back to Australia
again. The waves started to wash over the sides and drench
whoever was rowing. The massive outlines of ships crisscrossing
the horizon now appeared regularly as we found ourselves in
the middle of a shipping lane.

The wind and sea picked up so much as to make it
impossible to make any headway when rowing. It felt like we
were stuck in a vortex. We were being drenched by the steep
seas without being able to move much in any direction. It was
still early days and neither of us had got into the rhythm of
being at sea, so those shifts were lonely ones. Sitting on the
rowing seat, in pain, waiting for the next wave to sluice over
the deck was tough; it was our first real experience of getting
wet and staying wet for hours on end. By the time night came
we decided that rowing was getting us nowhere, so we took
it in turns to sit out on deck keeping an eye out for ships.
Every time one of those hulking masses of steel bore down

on us we tried desperately to call them on the VHF and warn them of our position. Most responded and changed course, but others didn't and came so close that we could see their bridges lit up in the bleak night. To while away the hours on deck we listened to audio books on my iPod. Overnight we were pushed back about six miles.

The whole of the next day we remained stuck in the vortex, rowing for a couple of hours, going nowhere, then having a break to play magnetic scrabble. On the satellite phone we spoke to Tony who told us that the four-man team, who had left the day after us, were stuck in similar weather but were pushing north. He also told us that Roz Savage, a solo rower, who had left Fremantle a fortnight or so before, had taken a tow back to Australia as her watermaker had broken. She had previously crossed the Atlantic and Pacific, so had a huge amount of experience. This was nerve-racking news because our own watermaker was starting to play up. We'd run it for two hours a day, every day, without a problem, but it was now making a strange noise and failing to produce any water. We couldn't turn back. We would ration what we had left and, when the weather improved, try to fix it.

Later on Day 7 we were visited by another shark. With its rusty colouring, it looked like a small bronze whaler. Having circled us, it swam right next to the boat, its sandpaper skin brushing our side. Once again I rushed to film it, but it had gone. However, I got the chance to film another of the ocean's wonders: the storm petrel. These tiny birds always appear in rough weather, hence their name. They would take light steps over the water, dipping their beaks in to scoop up plankton. They were totally unfazed by the huge waves they danced amid, never getting caught by any of them. We, on the other hand, were sitting ducks. Every few minutes we were swamped by another wave. Some of them were so powerful they would spin the boat around 180 degrees. After this, it would take ten minutes to row her back round into position only to be hit by another wave. It was dispiriting but we bided our time, waiting for the conditions to change.

The next day, however, nothing changed. We were stuck in the vortex for another day, going nowhere, getting wet. With the boat so heavily laden with 120 days' worth of provisions she sat low in the water and this meant that, instead of buoyantly floating over the waves as she was designed to, she took the full impact. Coming off a shift at this time it was nearly impossible to get dry in the cabin and the stifling humidity made it an uncomfortable place.

With the watermaker still not working, we resorted to using ballast water to hydrate our freeze-dried meals. We carried 150 litres of ballast water to stabilise the boat. It was stowed in hatches down the centre line of the boat so that if she capsized the weight of the ballast water would bring her back up. The water came in plastic bottles so it could be drunk in an emergency, and it seemed we already had an emergency on our hands. We agreed that as soon as the weather calmed and we got off the shelf we'd have a proper go at fixing the watermaker.

17 Surf's Up!

> 'The boat going with such madness through the water
> that the lee oars could scarcely be worked rapidly
> enough to escape being torn from the row-locks.'
> Herman Melville, *Moby Dick*

It was with dread that I opened the cabin hatch on the morning
of Day 9. We'd been stuck in the vortex for three days, getting
smashed around by the steep seas, while being pushed slowly
backwards through an international shipping lane.

But from Ben's face I knew there'd been a change.

'We're surfing!' he shouted.

The sky was heavy with black rain clouds, but the sea was
behind us now. The currents and winds were pushing us west
with such force that we were surfing down the waves. It's hard
to describe the sheer exhilaration of surfing down big waves
in a tiny rowing boat. When the waves first appear they seem
as if they will swamp and possibly even roll the boat. But if
we kept the boat lined up to the wave then they would pick
us up and shoot us along with a loud whoosh. In these
conditions we didn't stop for any meals but instead took it in
turns to eat so that one person was always lining the boat up
to the next wave and rowing through the troughs.

Every time a rain cloud passed overhead it unloaded a brief,
refreshing torrent. Beneath us the sea was rolling steeply like a
series of valleys, so that we couldn't see very far beyond
the next few waves coming to pick us up. Back in the vortex

we had fallen into a kind of damp lethargy, but now the adrenaline was pumping as we were suddenly flying along at three to four knots. We clearly had very strong currents beneath us as well as waves to surf – we were maintaining two knots even in the troughs of the waves. In four hours we rowed eighteen miles. We were on a high, enjoying the surfing so much that instead of resting in the cabin we'd sit out on deck to experience the rush of skidding wildly down the curving waves.

Then in the afternoon a small, yellow plane appeared. It flew low over us, then banked and flew past again. What did it mean? Had the coastguard found out about our watermaker failing and come to insist on rescuing us? Would they say it was too dangerous to continue through the endless valleys of waves? Had the police told them about my unpaid driving fine? My heart sank; somehow I thought it was all over. I rushed into the cabin and switched on the VHF radio.

'Aeroplane, aeroplane, aeroplane, this is *Indian Runner*, *Indian Runner*, *Indian Runner*, is there a problem, over?'

'*Indian Runner*, this is the West Australian Coastguard, please advise your home port and route, over.'

'Our home port is London and our route is Geraldton to Port Louis, Mauritius, over.'

'Mauritius! Good on ya. Well, this is just a routine exercise so good luck, boys.'

It was a false alarm; we were fine to carry on.

Although we didn't stop to eat our meals together in the surfing conditions, we still sat out on deck, chatting and, in the evening, we drank some whisky and smoked a cigarette each. By the end of the day we'd covered a record fifty-three miles. We assumed our new-found speed was partly because we had made it off the shelf, but it would be another forty-five days before we rowed that far in a day again.

* * *

The evening of Day 9 was particularly tough. We both struggled, in our own ways, with the steering of the boat. Ben has always had unbelievably poor eyesight and has always refused to wear glasses. In daylight he could never quite make out the compass, so during the night he really struggled to see where we were going as the compass was illuminated only by a very dim red light. I had issues with the foot-steering system, which was simply two ropes connecting the rudder to a moveable footplate. Every time a strong wave knocked into the rudder it yanked the footplate down because my foot wasn't able to hold it in one position and we were consequently thrown off course. It was deeply frustrating, like being slapped constantly in the face. Each time it happened I had to lean forward and pull the footplate back in line with my hands and then row like a maniac with one oar to line us up again. It was tiring, as well as humiliating, but whenever these kinds of conditions conspired to highlight my physical problems they made me all the more determined to keep going so as to prove a point, prove that I could do it. The inspiration to do the rowing had always been to have a great adventure, but the motivation to carry it through when things got tough was to prove people wrong, to make a statement about my abilities.

So there we were, on the morning of Day 10, one of us too blind to see the compass and the other unable to steer the boat in rough seas. We made a right pair. We needed a solution and the one I came up with was for me to steer with hand-lines instead of the footplate. So I sat in the rowing position and pulled on two pieces of rope as necessary to line up the boat. We still seemed to be going fast enough and because I wasn't rowing I had the energy to do it all day. It was unbelievable fun, like being in a chariot – after surfing each wave I would whip the ropes as if they were reins before the next wave catapulted us forward with a whoosh. The only problem was that the currents had by now deserted us and while we were making good speed in the waves we were stationary in the troughs. By the end of the day we had only done twenty-one miles, so we realised, with some regret, that we wouldn't be able to hand steer the whole way and would have to row across the ocean after all.

18 'Water'

'Water, water, every where,
And all the boards did shrink;
Water, water, every where,
Nor any drop to drink.'
Samuel Taylor Coleridge, *The
Rime of the Ancient Mariner*

The next few days were hard going, with the large swells that travel up unhindered from the Southern Ocean making for an uncomfortable ride. However, we still managed to average thirty-five miles a day. On the night of Day 11 we had a close call with a Chinese cargo ship that only changed its course after a fraught radio conversation.

With more items breaking on the boat we were developing a long 'to do' list, waiting for a calm day to mend everything. Foremost of these was, of course, the watermaker. With the watermaker down we were relying on the plastic bottles of ballast water which, after we'd drunk from them, we filled with sea water, marked and put back in the hold.

On Day 13 we tried to repressurise the watermaker, as Tony had shown us in Geraldton. It didn't work, and we went into the night shift dejected at the thought of having to use the hand pump. I was especially down at the prospect of having to manually pump our drinking water for the next three months. That night we were thrown around by violent seas and were forced to clip on for safety after one breaking wave spun us around more than 180 degrees.

The next day we tried again to repressurise, but again we failed to produce any water. Ben was being relentlessly positive about using the hand pump. 'It'll be fine,' he kept saying. 'We'll just do two hours' pumping each. Come on, nothing is going to stop us.' I couldn't help but think he wasn't imagining what it would really be like. I was full of dread at the prospect of using all that time and energy to produce some drinking water every single day for the next few months.

That night was calmer and cloudless; the night sky was breathtaking. I rowed my first shift under a canopy of stars that spun slowly through the sky. Shooting stars flashed across the night while satellites cruised methodically in and out of my vision. I thought about the reality of pumping, of an extra two hours' physical labour, which also meant two hours' less rest. But I decided Ben was right, nothing was going to stop us; the harder the row, the more wondrous finishing it would be. The beauty of this night, this was why we had come, and we couldn't turn back now. When Ben came out for his shift I reported my change of heart and the next day we started pumping.

Our situation felt immediately better now that we had a plan and had taken action. It was far worse to drink the ballast water each day while thinking about and dreading the pumping. When we actually started, it felt like we had a whole new purpose, a solution to what had seemed a near-intractable problem.

The physical act of pumping was tiring but not, as some people had suggested, worse than rowing. Two hours gives you about five litres so you have to pump for four hours to get the same amount that the electric machine would yield in two. However, there was an upside to the pumping. We had, up until this point, mainly rested in the cabin if we weren't rowing.

This meant that you were nearly always on your own, either rowing or sleeping. We would normally have a quick chat about what the weather or boat was doing, much like in cricket when an incoming batsman will pause to talk with the outgoing batsman about the bowling or wicket. Apart from this, there was little in the way of conversation as the tired rower made a dash for the cabin. We were like ships passing in the night. But doing the pumping outside meant we would spend four hours on deck together chatting.

These water-pumping sessions became one of the highlights of the trip. One day we'd mind-map St Andrews, stopping to reminisce about each pub or discuss each shop. How did the Christmas Shop on Market Street survive in the summer? This was one of the great questions that we debated. We also argued about films. Ben always championed big budget American blockbusters with apocalyptic scenarios while I spoke up for pretentious art-house films with subtitles. Then we spent hours picking our fantasy rugby teams. Categories included sides for ocean rowers, British politicians, actors, musicians and dictators. This provided endless hours of entertainment as we compared the relative scrummaging pedigrees of, say, Brian Blessed for the Actors against John Prescott for the Politicians. A number of theoretical problems would arise; for example, would Hitler, as captain of the Dictators, be able to see beyond his prejudice to select Idi Amin as a number 8? Of course, we also briefly discussed serious matters: life, love, careers, navigation and all that stuff . . . but mainly we talked rubbish.

19 On Our Way

'Already we are boldly launched upon the deep; but soon we shall be lost in its un-shored, harbourless immensities.'

Herman Melville, *Moby Dick*

We woke up on Day 15 to news that Osama bin Laden had been shot and buried at sea in the Indian Ocean. Incidentally, Bin Laden had controversially been included as a full-back for the Dictators XV despite his status as an actual dictator being in dispute. It was strange receiving texts on our satellite phone with such major international news. Each day we would receive a weather update from Tony, along with messages from our girlfriends and other friends. Hearing about events like Bin Laden's death made us feel far away from the 'real world', as if the world we were in was somehow very unreal. As time went on this perception changed, and our world felt more real and more important, or at least just as important and meaningful as the one we'd left behind.

Time, we came to realise, is a very different phenomenon at sea. Now we spent as much time awake at night as we spent sleeping and the idea of conventional patterns to the day lost its meaning. Typically we would row two hours on then two hours off during the day and three hours on/off at night. On dry land you become used to sleeping at night and working during the day, which means that the distinction between the two becomes very marked. After the regular routines of dry land, our seafaring routine served to make the days feel short and the nights long. If it was a majestic, calm night this was a new and beautiful discovery but if it was a rough, starless night it was an ordeal. In the end it became irrelevant what time it was; the only thing that mattered was what the weather was like. If the weather was good, time disappeared and days flew by, but in rough, adverse conditions a three-hour shift could feel like a day.

As for sleeping, it was never a problem nodding off because we were so tired from the rowing. We quickly got used to sleeping for only a few hours at a time because we would be sleeping more than once throughout each 24-hour period. There were occasions, though, when one person would over-sleep. At first we were polite, so you might hear a voice in the darkness saying, 'Err, mate, I think it's your turn now because it's, umm, five minutes past.' As our journey advanced, this gave way to, 'Your go!' and, eventually, 'Get out here now, you lazy bastard!'

We were now two weeks in and land had become a distant memory as we adjusted to our new, watery world. We had strong south-easterlies blowing us along but, wary of going too far north, we were forced to row on a beam sea, which meant we were constantly being hit by waves from the side. In hindsight, it might have been better to ride the weather north in more comfort and in the knowledge that the currents and winds from the north would take us back on course in the second half. But we didn't have this knowledge and were reliant on Tony for information. He, in turn, only had the 2009 crossings to go on, and our course was already diverging from theirs.

Our bodies were deteriorating at this stage. The claw hand was with us at the beginning of every shift, although the pain would go away after about ten minutes. Our bums were in agony, too. The constant damp kept the skin soft while the endless rowing wore it down. Salt sores were becoming a problem and they marked those parts of the body where the sun doesn't shine (unless you were to employ some of Ben's more experimental stretching techniques). We would take it in turns to stand up by the cabin door while the other person was rowing, pull down our cycling shorts and enquire, 'How does it look today?' To which the rower, narrowing his eyes and wincing, would reply in as convincing a manner as possible, 'Much better than yesterday, buddy,' or some such lie. Sitting down at the start of a shift was very painful and rowing on a beam sea even worse. Every time the boat rocked from side to side our weight would shift its entirety onto each buttock, prompting bouts of shout-out-loud swearing. These were our standard afflictions, but we also had other problems – athlete's foot, constipation, diarrhoea – you name it, we had it.

Two weeks in and it took all our energies to keep up with the still unfamiliar routine. We really needed our food and consequently we were really enjoying it. There were still meals that we couldn't stomach and they went back into the storage holds below the deck, but we had by then identified some clear favourites. One of these was lamb pilaf. Our love of this lamb dish and our bodily exhaustion led to the infamous 'Lamb Pilaf Incident'. Ben was on deck and had just finished boiling the water for his lunch, a prized sachet of delicious freeze-dried lamb pilaf. Just as he added the water his claw hand seized and he dropped the meal, scalding his foot and spilling half of it on deck. In a rage he flung the remainder of the meal overboard, straight into the strong south-easterly wind, which in turn blew it in my direction, caking my face in pilaf. Not wanting to further antagonise him, I wordlessly wiped the food off my face, but thereafter I'd often ask him if we were about to have another lamb pilaf moment.

20 Swim

'Now, in calm weather, to swim in the open ocean
is as easy to the practiced swimmer as to ride in a
spring-carriage ashore. But the awful lonesomeness
is intolerable. The intense concentration of self in
the middle of such a heartless immensity, my God!
Who can tell it?'

Herman Melville, *Moby Dick*

On Day 17 the swell died down and at noon, under blue skies,
we were able to have our first swim. Ben went first and I
filmed the moment on one of our cameras. The sun cast shafts
of light deep into the blue. It was surreal watching Ben pause
on the side of the boat and then jump in wearing nothing
but a mask.

'It's amazing!' he shouted. 'It's so refreshing.'

I passed him some of our saltwater washing liquid and he
washed his hair. Clouds of white shampoo drifted down,
billowing slowly into the depths.

Then it was my turn. By this stage we were four hundred
miles out to sea and we knew from our charts that we were
in over five thousand metres of water. I've always loved
swimming in the sea but there was something unnerving,
almost unnatural, about jumping into water this deep. I
plunged in wearing the mask and sank deep into the
cavernous ocean. Tumbling down, I had a strange sense of
vertigo as if my body instinctually knew the awesome depth
of this sea.

I'd dived in many countries but I'd never had visibility like this before; the rays of sunlight illuminated the deep in an eerie, endless way. It was the blue of eternity, like looking at the sky. Inspecting the hull of the boat, I saw we already had a build-up of marine growth and, darting in and around the hull, boisterously swimming up to me, were five tiny pilot fish.

Pilot fish are so called because they accompany ships on long passages, seemingly piloting them across oceans. They have black and white stripes and are amazingly tame; they would often swim up and nibble on my hand as I dipped it into the water. We decided to name the larger ones after our girlfriends and I knew it would please Tory to have her aquatic namesake joining us across the Indian Ocean. That day we spoke on the satellite phone and it was a real boost to hear her voice and hear her enthusiasm for the latest developments in our floating world.

That night we had a swig of Calvados and a ciggie and were treated to another stunning evening with the sky so clear the shooting stars appeared to explode as they hit the atmosphere, trailing long wakes like lightning.

At dawn I opened the hatch at the back of the aft cabin and stood there, taking a pee into a sea gold with the most incredible sunrise. In the sky clouds hung motionless, on fire with the red of the rising sun, which was just now showing its glowing crescent.

'You still here?' I shouted, not turning round. I could hear the rhythmic dip and pull of the oars behind me.

'Yup,' Ben replied.

'Amazing, isn't it?'

'Best one yet.'

We were starting to get into the rhythm of life at sea. We

were in pain but more and more we were able to take in and appreciate our surroundings. My body was getting used to the routine and I felt as if I was coming round after the madness of the last few weeks and waking up in the most beautiful place imaginable.

21 Another Rower

> 'In the maritime life, far more than on terra firma, wild rumours abound, whenever there is any adequate reality for them to cling to.'
>
> Herman Melville, *Moby Dick*

On Day 18 we were back to battling away in rough seas. We were doing good miles but it was uncomfortable going. In the afternoon we spoke to Tony on the satellite phone. He warned us that we'd have strong winds for another week but he also had a fascinating snippet of news. He told us that a guy called Keith had not long left Geraldton in an attempt to row across the Indian solo. This was an extraordinary development. I had heard Keith's name a few months back as someone who might be attempting the Indian at the same time as us. I'd forgotten about it because he didn't have a boat and, as we'd learnt, people don't take you seriously until you at least have a boat.

But here we were a month or so later, in the middle of the ocean, hearing the news that Keith had left Australia. All Tony could tell us was that Keith had somehow rented Rob Eustace's boat. The last time we'd seen Rob's boat it had been on a trailer being driven down to Fremantle by Rob himself. Talk about the Irish having the gift of the gab. 'Who the hell is this Keith guy?' we asked each other in amazement.

We were divided on the answer to this question. Ben was generally in favour of Keith. He thought you had to hand it to him for being so bold, pioneering and lucky. He admired Keith's brazen, last minute dash for glory. Ben reckoned he was a sort of Irish Simon Chalk. To my mind he was very different from Simon. Okay, I could see there was a certain marauding charm about him, and his obvious lunacy struck a chord, too, but there was one vital difference for me. It had everything to do with preparation. I didn't think it was fair that he turned up at the start line, got straight into Rob's meticulously prepared boat and set off. We'd spent years saving and the best part of a year planning, preparing, filling out forms, running around the country buying second-hand kit, organising shipping, sponsorship – you name it, we'd done it and done it what felt like the hard way. Apart from being rattled by this sense of injustice, I thought it unlikely that anyone could complete the Indian in such a cavalier fashion. By way of contrast, the sheer scale of all the preparations was a huge motivation for us. All that time, money and effort were still in the forefront of my mind when we set off. There was no way I'd let us turn back, fail, no matter what happened to us.

To turn up at such short notice and set off in someone else's boat that they'd prepared seemed akin to doing a 'pay-per-place' row. 'Pay-per-place' is when people pay a fee to row in a ten- or twelve-man boat. It has become a popular way to cross the Atlantic as it means people can have the experience of rowing an ocean at minimal cost and without all the hassle of organising it themselves. The only drawback is spending upwards of a month in very close quarters with 11 strangers. On a boat like that you are never alone; you row with others, sleep with others and when it's time to sit on the bucket to perform your daily ablutions you do it in front of others. No doubt it's a great experience in its own way, but it was never what I imagined when dreaming about rowing an ocean.

At the same time as updating us about Keith's departure Tony also told us that Roz Savage had left from Geraldton in her second attempt to row the Indian solo. We had read about Roz, a world record holder, who had already rowed solo across the Atlantic and Pacific. She is a supreme athlete, a vocal eco-warrior and has a formidable PR campaign. She had originally left from Fremantle but had failed to make any decent headway despite battling away for ten days or so, and had to come back in after her watermaker broke.

It was hard imagining her and Keith setting off at a similar time; they were such contrasting characters. As were Simon, Rob, the four-man crew and all the other ocean rowers we had met. What, we wondered, had all these disparate people in common?

22 On the Personalities Drawn to Ocean Rowing

'Nowadays, the whale-fishery furnishes an asylum
for many romantic, melancholy, and absent-minded
young men, disgusted with the carking cares of
earth, and seeking sentiment in tar and blubber.'
Herman Melville, *Moby Dick*

Back in Geraldton we had asked Simon if he ever got fed up
with all the complaints about Woodvale he got from ocean
rowers; we knew there had been various issues in previous
races. 'The sort of people who row oceans tend to be very
highly strung,' he'd replied. From what we had seen he was
right; the ocean rowers we'd met tended to be fiercely
independent, emotional, highly motivated and very cavalier
about personal safety.

In our opinion, most ocean rowers fall into two categories
(although there is always some overlap). First there are the
endurance rowers. These are the people who see rowing an ocean
as the ultimate physical challenge. For them it's a kind of aquatic
Ironman during which Mother Nature will throw everything
she has at them and they have to use their strength and ingenuity
to succeed. They place great emphasis on training and nutrition.
They also tend to excel at fundraising and are relatively sensible
people, which is to say sensible within the parameters of ocean
rowing. Breaking records normally appeals to these rowers and
they see the activity very much as a sport.

Then there are the romantic rowers. For them it's all about the journey. Being at sea is the ultimate reward. They tend to distance themselves from any record attempts, normally in the knowledge that their haphazard training regimes have slipped by the wayside as they rather chaotically prepare for their row. Being romantic, they've spent a lot of time dreaming and not enough time planning. While the endurance rowers prepare for the worst the romantics often idealise the voyage, imagining it as some sort of spiritual journey. Time is on their side as they are often fleeing unsatisfactory employment or relationships. If not these, then they are escaping some other aspect of modern life. As Theodore Rezvoy, who was rescued after nineteen days on the Indian, said, 'On the ocean there are no cars, no television, no bills and no police.'

We often joked that the reason Simon spent so much of his time (a total of 313 days) at sea, in a small rowing boat, with limited contact with the outside world, was that he was on the run from the police. In some ways it was unfair to say that he went to sea to avoid the chaos of his business and other affairs, but we couldn't help but understand this aspect of his motivation. Hadn't we originally thought of rowing an ocean as an escape from the drudgery of our lives in London?

Whatever category they fell into, the ocean rowers we met always had a story and we spent a lot of time discussing all the different characters we'd met. Whenever Ben and I had a difference of opinion we'd make up bits of philosophy or quotations from various ocean rowers to prove our point.

So Ben might say, 'Stop whingeing. Keith famously never takes toilet paper to sea.' To which I'd reply, 'Yes, but Simon is renowned for always taking at least ten sheets per person per day on his trips.'

We joked, but we had a lot of time for the ocean rowers we met. It was striking how unconventional, fascinating and, indeed, highly strung they all were. We knew of, and had met, a lot of people who had fallen out on rowing boats. The clash of strong personalities, in a confined space, in such testing conditions was sometimes so extreme that they didn't speak again after getting back to dry land. We'd heard about a four-man boat on the Indian where an argument had led to one of the crew hiding in the forward cabin and refusing to come out for three days. We were aware of these more personal dangers and were determined not to fall into the trap of blaming each other – not to mention getting nasty, petulant or spiteful – when things went wrong. But of course anything can happen at sea.

23 Timothy and the Filofax

'We are merely the stars' tennis-balls, struck and
banded which way please them.'
John Webster, *The Duchess of Malfi*

Day 21 found us arguing. Not seriously, but in our usual ironic
fashion. I was trying to convince Ben to throw his leather
Filofax overboard. He had forced me to chuck a pair of chinos,
which for some reason I had worn the day we left. We didn't
get splashed for the first four hours and I kept saying, 'The
chinos still aren't wet, they're proving to be a great bring.'
But then we got drenched and the chinos quickly went in. Ben,
on the other hand, had insisted on bringing his Filofax, an
organisational tool that went out of fashion in the late 1980s.
It was massive and there wasn't even anything in it; I had all
our important documents in a waterproof wallet. Ben had
been putting up a big fight for three weeks, so attached was
he to this relic. He tried to turn the tables on me saying I
should throw overboard my 'Aladdin pants', as he called the
lightweight, baggy trousers I had brought from India, although
his concerns here were more visual than spacial. But we were
so overloaded with stuff that finally he agreed the Filofax had
to go. I filmed the occasion and the eulogy Ben gave his Filofax
as it drifted off like a melancholy Viking funeral ship.

Around lunchtime, still coming to terms with his loss, Ben
decided to call his mum on the satellite phone. He was standing
up by the aft cabin with his back to me while I was rowing.

We were seven hundred miles out to sea. All signs of land had disappeared, there was no seaweed in the water and our only companions were the pilot fish and seabirds. Then the most extraordinary thing happened. A tiny moth landed on Ben's back. Here we were, seven hundred miles from the nearest land, and a moth was flying around. When Ben finished on the phone we inspected him, deciding that he was a normal moth, not some kind of sea moth we'd never heard of. He'd clearly been blown off course or had lost his way chasing the full moon. We named him Timothy and put him in the cabin. Tim, we agreed, was our friend and he was coming all the way to Mauritius with us.

Things were still tough at this stage. We were desperate for a calm day in which to carry out all the repairs. Our jet boil (which was used for boiling the water that hydrated our food) had broken, so we were on our backup, only cooking inside to preserve it; our satellite phone had mysteriously broken (probably due to moisture or salt water getting into it somehow) so we were using the backup, again inside only; the rowlocks still kept coming loose; our bodies were aching and we were tiring of pumping our own water. In short, it was starting to feel like we were losing control.

Another worrying development was how low the boat was sitting in the water. One evening in particular she was sagging so low that I became convinced we were sinking. We swam under the boat to investigate and couldn't see any obvious holes, but this did nothing to settle my anxieties.

On the morning of Day 22 we opened the cabin door and, after only one night of sleeping in the cabin, Tim flew away. It seemed that he preferred certain death at sea to spending any more time with us. It felt like a bad omen.

At night we were trialling longer shifts to give the other

person a chance of more rest. The extra sleep helped, but four hours on was a long time to row and in bad weather it could get particularly lonely. Small setbacks had a dramatic effect. For example, halfway through one of my four-hour shifts I made a hot chocolate and sat down to drink it. I'd spent the first two hours fantasising about it, working towards it. As I lifted the steaming sweetness to my lips a wave crashed over the side, swamping my drink. This sort of incident could ruin a night shift. But one of my worst lows came a few nights later. I had with me an iPod filled with audio books. I'd spent a lot of time downloading long novels and histories and we both found that listening to these helped get us through the darker nights. But one night I discovered that the salt water had got to the iPod, killing it. I was, for a while, inconsolable, despite having another iPod full of music.

'Don't worry; remember I've also got an iPod you can use,' said Ben, in an effort to pacify my dark mood.

'But you've only got a hundred and twenty-six songs on it and most of them are by Celine Dion,' I complained.

'Oh come on, she's done some great work.'

Apart from a small selection of early 1990s ballads Ben isn't that bothered about music, whereas it has always held a lot of significance for me. Some of my favourite times on the water were listening to music. It always filled me with joy when a fitting song came on, like the time when Israel Kamakawiwo's cover of 'Somewhere Over the Rainbow' came on while we were rowing through a succession of rainbows, or when Dire Straits' 'Sultans of Swing' played while we skipped along at three knots under a full moon. Sometimes it could be incongruous, like when Hans Zimmer's atmospheric soundtrack to *Inception* played during a storm, creating the sense that I was trapped in some weird, never-ending nightmare. Other times it was ironic, The Kinks' 'Sunny

Afternoon' in a rainstorm, or sometimes just downright odd, like the morning I got drum and bass during a serene sunrise.

Either way, the iPods made the difficult times much more bearable and I really felt the loss of the audio books at this early stage. Later I would have to learn to live without music as well.

24 The First Becalming

'So strange a dreaminess did there reign all over the ship and the sea.'

Herman Melville, *Moby Dick*

Throughout the morning of Day 27 the swell was dying down to small ripples and by lunch there was nothing but a glassy still. There wasn't a whisper of wind or swell, which had the extraordinary effect of making the sea as calm as a swimming pool. The surface of the sea was so flat it acted like a mirror reflecting back the blue of the sky and white of the low clouds that hung motionless above us.

It was the calm day we'd been waiting for those past few weeks, but when it came its surreal beauty was surprising. I'd come to think of the ocean as being only capable of movement. There had always been waves or swell up until this point and we'd always been moving backwards or forwards, north or south. But as we stopped rowing at lunch and checked the GPS it confirmed that we were completely stationary. It was an amazing feeling, being eight hundred miles out to sea but suddenly in calm, millpond conditions.

The silence when we stopped rowing was overwhelming and bizarre. Normally the boat would always be making a noise, gurgling and creaking as she moved through the water, waves tapping against the hull, the oars and the seat sliding back and forth. But now there was nothing and for the first time I experienced the truth of the phrase 'deafening silence'.

Peering into the gin-clear ocean, it was impossible to gauge the depth unless something, like a spoonful of lunch, was sinking down into the impenetrable blue. It was possible to see tiny individual plankton floating like planets through the eternal sea. Some were perfectly round, expanding and contracting as they drifted past while others were long like pieces of hair. These were the organisms that lit up at night in such spectacular flashes of green and gold when our oars touched them, and they were everywhere.

We set to work on all the jobs that needed doing. When we checked all the holds where our food was stored in waterproof bags we discovered that a huge amount of water had leaked in. We pumped it out by hand, counting over a hundred litres. No wonder the boat had been sagging so sluggishly. It was incredible how high she sat in the water after we had finished. We agreed that we would have to pump out the seven holds that sat underneath the deck every few days from now on. After tackling the other repairs we managed to speak to a watermaker specialist called Jim MacDonald on the satellite phone. He talked us through a way of repairing our electric watermaker. We replaced the pressure relief valve and bled the air out of the system then we started to make sweet, sweet water. We were now on a massive high, we'd worked so hard pumping our own water but now here was a machine to do it for us.

With the watermaker running and the other repairs done, we decided to take the rest of the day off. We took it in turns to swim. I took the film camera in and swam in a big circle around the boat. I swam about twenty metres from the boat but, even without the slightest hint of wind, it felt uncomfortable to go any further. She looked so small and insignificant on the wide sea, which stretched away in every direction, untroubled, until it merged with the horizon. But I felt confident in her.

She had been battered by some fierce seas and had stood up to the test. I pointed the camera down, filming my toes pointing into the cavernous vacuum of blue.

Bizarrely, Paddington was still standing strong on the prow, suitcase intact, wellington boots still firmly on. The bear was clearly going the whole way.

Finally we took it in turns to clean the hull with a metal scraper to get rid of the barnacles. It was amazing how much marine growth had accumulated in such a short time but then in this, the harshest and most symbiotic of environments, the fastest of whales host barnacles and the sleekest of sharks carry their cleaner wrasse.

Back on board we had a wash and then lay down, one on either gunwale, drifting in and out of sleep in the warm afternoon sun.

Later we had a call from a family friend of mine, Nick Eyles, an experienced sailor who had given us lots of help before we set off. He had seen from the tracking that we had slowed to a halt and wanted to know if everything was okay.

'Absolutely,' I said, 'couldn't be better.' He had spoken to the Met Office and the forecast was good; it sounded like we'd be surfing again in a couple of days. We decided to take the night off, to rest our bodies and prepare mentally for the next weather system. 'Anyway,' we said to each other, 'we're not trying to break any records, we're just here for the experience and we feel like taking a night off.' Having justified ourselves, we decided on a feast for dinner, no freeze-dried food, instead we would eat some of the treats we had packed. Under a setting sun we tucked into pork scratchings, tins of tuna, pineapple chunks and two chocolate bars each for dessert. This simple fare tasted exquisite after all the freeze-dried food; the textures of each component were subtle and pleasing and it was as if our bodies were begging for what they offered in oil and fat and freshness.

That night we rearranged the cabin so we could both sleep at the same time, opting to top and tail as opposed to the more intimate spooning we had unwisely attempted during the violent seas of the vortex. Then we slept a deep, long sleep, like hibernating bears. By the time we woke up in the morning our salt sores had greatly improved and we felt like different people. One unbroken sleep had made us feel like new.

The next day was Day 28, which meant we had been at sea four weeks. I was beginning to love our life at sea, watching the ever-changing ocean and immensity of the heavens. I now only experienced pain in my hands or arse at the beginning of each shift, and within ten minutes it was gone. I felt completely fit and could easily row for three hours without stopping. Also, it didn't seem like we'd lost much weight. It felt like we'd had an almighty battle to get to this stage, but that everything was getting better: the watermaker was fixed, the weather was calmer and we were seeing more wildlife every day.

water only to scare themselves when they got too close. They loved to jump. Every day that they were with us, they would leap three or four feet into the air in an outlandish display of strength. Often they would perform a series of jumps in which they would go higher and higher before belly-flopping hard on the final fling. I wasn't sure if they were trying to rid themselves of parasites, practise hunting or if they were performing some kind of mating ritual with these fantastic acrobatics. Later in our journey, as I sat silently rowing through their world, it seemed as if they might be showing off to us.

The flying fish they pursued were equally fascinating, although harder to observe because they were forever soaring away from the dorado. The flying fish announced themselves in a big way on Day 16. I was rowing quietly along when a huge one launched itself from the surface of the sea, about three metres from the boat, taking a flight path directly towards my face. I'm not sure who was more surprised, but it was probably the fish. It can't often happen in an ocean virtually deserted by men and boats that a flying fish takes flight and actually finds something in its path. I managed to lean back just in time to avoid the collision, feeling him whoosh by my face as I fell backwards off the seat.

It seems appropriate that the family name of this fish, Exocoetidae, gave its name to the Exocet missile. Later on there were quite a few direct hits to the boat and even one to the body when a flying fish hit me on the arm.

One of our frequent debates on the boat was whether these fish could actually fly or whether what they did was just a glorified glide. As we progressed, we witnessed some impressive flight times and distances. So often the fish seemed to be deliberately riding the winds or thermals as they escaped their predators. We decided that if they can't actually 'fly' then they could be termed 'serial gliders'; we observed that as they came to the end of one flight they often flicked their tail on a wave so as to take flight again before entering the water. This classification would put them above more basic gliders, such as flying foxes, which can only manage one flight at a time from one tree to another. We tried to count the flight times of the fish when they breached but they usually disappeared from sight before re-entering the water. The longest recorded flight time is 45 seconds, which was captured by a Japanese film crew.

The dorado and the flying fish were with us all the way. At first it felt like we were trespassing in their strange world but as our journey wore on it felt more like we were all trying to survive the unforgiving sea together.

26 Storm

'The mind jettisoned everything that might prove harmful to it, since a thing that is of no use can only be harmful. Only the animal instinct which remains hidden deep inside each one of us had risen to the surface, there to exaggerate its dimensions, take complete possession of the boat-man unit, and impose on it the only order that made any sense; to hang on, whatever happens – hang on.'

Bernard Moitessier, *Sailing to the Reefs*

After the brief respite of the first becalming, we were hit with our first storm. The weather built over the course of Day 29 and during that night we were hit by a big wave while I was balancing on the side, taking a leak. The boat shuddered and lurched onto its side. I managed not to fall overboard but couldn't stop what I'd started and so pissed all over myself. This trick of balancing on the gunwales to answer the call of nature was, we eventually discovered by Day 60, far too dangerous. We'd both fallen in in such circumstances, but luckily both incidents were in daylight while the other person was on deck to help. Accuracy in high winds presented another problem; it was after a disastrous attempt to piss into 25 knots of wind blowing in the direction of the other rower that 'the bottle' was instigated, which greatly improved matters.

We used surfboard straps to clip onto the boat in rough weather, which mitigated the danger of falling in at night; if we had ended up in the sea the combination of exhaustion and strong currents could have been fatal. However, we did become, if not blasé, then more confident in the boat and in each other's ability to survive the night. At first, when you were rowing along in the dark and a big wave hit, the cabin door would open and the other person would sleepily say something like, 'Are you okay, that sounded like a really big one, are you sure you're alright?' But after a few weeks, the massive night-time waves failed to provoke a response; the cabin door would remain tightly shut and you'd carry on rowing, muttering to yourself, 'Here I am rowing away and he doesn't care whether I live or die.'

If you were the sleeper the scenario went like this. At first you'd hear the wave hit, which always sounded much louder in the cabin, and you'd think, How did we survive that? I better check he is still there. But after a few weeks you were so tired that, after the crashing wave woke you up and the rowing ominously stopped, you would think to yourself, I'll just wait until I hear him rowing again to make sure he's alive. Ah, there's the sound of him swearing and, yes, there are the oars going again, he must be okay, and you'd promptly fall straight back to sleep. Having said this, it was our constant nightmare that one dark night we'd come out of the cabin to find that the other person wasn't there.

The weather was worsening on Day 30 and, during my off shifts, while listening to music and watching Ben getting drenched by waves, I would count down the hours and minutes before it was my turn. On days like this we always entered the night shifts with a sense of dread. The first night shift was mine, so as the sun disappeared I was left battling increasingly violent seas and lashing rain. We were constantly being hit by large breaking waves and the boat was filling up, so every twenty minutes I would precariously crawl from the rowing position to the bilge pump to empty the deck. Back in the rowing position, it was virtually impossible to point the boat in the right direction because of the strength of the wind behind us and the state of the sea, which was churning like a washing machine. The outlines of the waves were visible only at the last moment before they hit us. The constant din of the storm raged all around. I kept thinking to myself, Is this safe? I had nothing to compare it to, so it was hard to judge, but I thought probably not. However, not wanting to get it wrong or give up too easily I sat it out until the end of my shift. A couple of hours later Ben came out in his foul weather gear and crouched on the deck ready to take over. We were right next to each other, but he had to shout to be heard: 'What are you doing? It's definitely not safe to be out here!' So we locked down the oars and got into the relative safety of the cabin to top and tail for a stifling night. At one point I clambered out to go to the loo amid the mad, mountainous, moonlit waves. In the cabin our fatigue got the better of our fear and we were easily able to sleep despite the swell slamming loudly into the sides of the boat. When we emerged next morning we were thrilled to discover that we had been blown forward ten miles.

27 Catch 22

'I hate storms but calms undermine my spirits.'
Bernard Moitessier, *The Long Way*

The following night I was once again rowing the first night shift and as we rolled along I could see flashes of lightning in the distance in front of us. At first it seemed like we were heading straight towards another storm and, terrified, I'd look back over my right shoulder every few minutes to see the erratic forks of lightning silently illuminating the distant sky. The jagged shards of light seemed to be reaching the sea to the south of us. But it soon became apparent that we would miss the storm by a long way, which made it easier to enjoy the natural fireworks display.

With following seas, which is when the waves and wind come from behind the boat, we were flying along again. We recorded our top speed, an exhilarating 12.5 knots in one wave. Surfing these waves was without a doubt the most brilliant fun, but the drawback to such speed was the general lack of comfort that accompanied it. In this sort of weather we would cover good miles and the rowing was exciting, but everything would get wet, and sleeping in a damp and pitching cabin was not fun.

On Day 36 Tony reported that we were now 39 nautical miles ahead of where the record holders had been in 2009. In contrast to the four-man team we had been quite vocal before we left about *not* aiming for any records. From our limited under-standing of ocean rowing, we suspected that pace all depended on the weather you got – and this certainly turned out to be true for us. Also, from a psychological point of view, we thought that aiming for a record could ruin our enjoyment of a once-in-a-lifetime voyage by making us liable to worry every day about how we were comparing to two different people, in a different boat, rowing the ocean in different weather back in 2009. On top of this the simple fact is that not many people have rowed oceans, so there's nearly always some kind of record to claim. We'd heard some ridiculous ones and we'd amuse ourselves by coming up with new outlandish records we could claim such as the first lapsed, inter-faith (Catholic–CofE) crossing of the Indian Ocean; the first pairs crossing of an ocean to be done in total silence; the first crossing of the Indian Ocean conducted only in French by non-native French speakers; the most number of cumulative days spent not rowing during an ocean row; the record for the pair carrying the most non-essential supplies; the most books read whilst rowing an ocean; or the record for the most claimed and rejected records in connection to an ocean row.

Of course, this isn't to say we weren't more than a little seduced by the idea of becoming the world record holders for the quickest pair's crossing of the Indian Ocean, especially if it came relatively easily. People back on dry land wouldn't understand that it was weather-dependent, wouldn't know that we were only up against two pairs who both rowed across in 2009 only a day apart. Maybe we'd get lucky with surfing conditions the whole way across, and people back home would think that we were superhuman athletes. This is what we'd discuss over our nightly brandy and cigarette. We imagined how, on Christmas Day, we could leave the Guinness Book of World Records handily open on the ocean rowing section when we'd achieved our record. Now that we were off the shelf and well on our way, we'd made a pretty big statement to all those who doubted we'd ever even attempt an ocean, but to go on and break the record would finish any arguments for good. So, telling ourselves that we weren't getting obsessed, we started to become a little bit more competitive. We stopped our short communal breaks for meals, so that now someone was always rowing, twenty-four hours a day. We started pushing ourselves harder – all in pursuit of something we believed to be illusory and meaningless, an ocean rowing world record.

28 A Brief History of Ocean Rowing

'But if adventure has a final and all embracing motive it is surely this: We go out because it is in our nature to go out, to climb mountains and to sail the seas, to fly to the planets and plunge into depths of the oceans. By doing these things we make touch with something outside or behind, which strangely seems to approve our doing them. We extend our horizon, we expand our being, we revel in the mastery of ourselves which gives an impression, mainly illusory, that we are masters of the World. In a word, we are men and when man ceases to do these things, he is no longer man.'

Wilfred Noyce

Just as ocean rowers can be categorised as endurance rowers and romantic rowers, so can ocean rows be split into historic and modern rows. The people who undertook the historic rows did so without a watermaker, GPS, satellite phone or any of the other kit now considered vital to an ocean crossing. In short, they were lunatics. In the words of Gérard d'Aboville, who rowed the Atlantic in 1980, 'We were like test pilots without a parachute.' Before all the modern equipment became available, teams would often accept assistance from passing boats or do their crossings in a series of legs, and the difficulty in corroborating or comparing these voyages has led to the historic/modern divide.

Historic

The first recorded ocean row took place in 1896 on the west to east North Atlantic route when two Norwegian-born American fishermen rowed from New York to the Scilly Isles. Harbo and Samuelson completed their feat in 55 days. The specially built eighteen-foot boat, called *The Fox*, was fitted with rails, which they used to right the boat when it capsized mid-ocean. At the end of their row, they were cheated out of their prize money by the very newspaper editor who had promoted the event. On the voyage home the ship ran out of coal and when the master ordered all wooden objects to be broken up and fed to the fire the pair decided to relaunch *The Fox* and row all the way back to New York just to preserve her. That's the Victorians for you. Their extraordinary voyage remained the quickest crossing for 114 years until a four-man crew beat it in 2010.

Nobody attempted another ocean row until 1966 when two British teams set out on the same route as Harbo and Samuelson. The first boat to leave was called *Puffin*, although tragically she was later lost at sea along with both crewmembers. Their last log entry was on Day 105. It's thought that they'd drunk their supplies of fresh water, which doubled as ballast, then failed to replace it with seawater. This left their boat unstable and it was later recovered upside-down, suggesting that the cause of death was mid-ocean capsize.

The second team to leave consisted of two soldiers, Chay Blyth and John Ridgeway, who completed the row in 92 days. They rowed into the history books and were feted at home. However, Blyth was uncompromising when asked about the fate of the *Puffin*. Citing his rivals' mistake of not replacing the ballast water, he said, 'I wouldn't even call it a tragedy. They made so many mistakes. The first one was publishing their plans, allowing others to dovetail right into them, which is exactly what we did. Then they changed their plans and for the worse. We got the idea to leave from Cape Cod from them, but then they started from Virginia to be closer to the Gulf Stream. It was a mistake. They had to cover about five hundred miles just to get to where we started . . . they didn't stick to the plan. If they had, they might be here today.'

The wild seas of the North Atlantic are a constant draw, although they are the most dangerous, with five of the seven rowers lost at sea dying on this route.

All the early ocean rowers were extraordinary characters. My personal favourite is John Fairfax, who in 1969 became the first person to row the Atlantic solo. Born in 1937 to a British father and Bulgarian mother, he was still young when he first got into trouble, booted out of the Boy Scouts for opening fire on the scout hut with a pistol following an argument with another boy. He moved to Argentina with his mother and not long after at the age of thirteen ran away to live in the jungle where, inspired by the *Tarzan* films, he lived by selling the furs of ocelots and jaguars he trapped. In his early twenties he inherited $10,000, upon which he flew to New York, bought a Chevrolet and drove to San Francisco. Here he took up with a Chinese call girl and, when his funds had dwindled to $150, decided to return to Argentina by bike. He got waylaid in Panama where he became a smuggler for a couple of years (taking a year out as a fisherman in Jamaica), before he had to flee after his involvement in a shoot-out. He returned to Argentina by horseback, where he briefly managed a mink farm before news of Ridgeway and Blyth's Atlantic crossing spurred him on to make his solo voyage.

Fairfax's Atlantic solo row took 180 days and saw him fight and kill a mako shark as well as board a passing cargo ship for a fry-up and a few beers. On completing his row, he received a message of congratulation from the crew of *Apollo 11*. In Florida, a journalist questioned the truth of his shark-fighting tales so Fairfax rented a boat, poured fish blood in the water and, when a suitable specimen turned up, leapt in, killed it and dumped the carcass on the journalist's doorstep.

Two years later he rowed the Pacific from San Francisco to Hayman Island, Australia, with his girlfriend, who couldn't swim. It took them 361 days with various stops. He later married another woman and lived out his days gambling as a baccarat expert in Las Vegas.

As cavalier as he was brave, the unconventional Fairfax embodied the spirit of the early ocean rowers. The few people who dared to row oceans between 1966 and 1982 pioneered the routes that would later be raced by the modern ocean rowers.

Modern

The first modern row was British adventurer Peter Bird's epic 294-day voyage from San Francisco to the Great Barrier Reef off the coast of Australia. This length of time at sea was only possible with a watermaker, and consequently the adjudicators of ocean rows, the Ocean Rowing Society, started standardising the criteria for an official row.

Still, only a trickle of independent rowers continued to cross oceans until, in 1997, Chay Blyth organised the inaugural Atlantic race with a business he would later sell to Simon Chalk, who would name it Woodvale. For the 1997 race, Blyth initiated an interesting rule that any abandoned boats would be torched in case they became a navigational hazard, so retiring crews had the double blow of watching their boat go up in smoke along with their dream.

The route, from the Canary Islands to the Caribbean, would become the standard route for rowers attempting the mid-Atlantic and, with official races on this route in 1997, 2001, 2003-2007, 2009 and 2011, it remains the most rowed of all oceans. Of the 329 boats that have thus far attempted this route, 247 have completed it. This figure includes solos, pairs, fours and larger pay-per-place crews.

Successful crossings of other oceanic routes have been less frequent, but teams have made it across the North Atlantic, North Pacific, Mid-Pacific and South Pacific, as well as the Indian. Other challenges have been completed, such as an Australia to New Zealand row and a race in stages around Britain. There have also been attempts to circumnavigate the world in a rowing boat by way of the treacherous Southern Ocean, but all have failed. This remains the most elusive prize in ocean rowing.

Unsurprisingly, the two men who have attempted a rowing circumnavigation are both experienced ocean rowers and both are British. The sport is dominated by the British, who are to ocean rowing what the Nantucketers were to whaling. Of the 519 people who have rowed an ocean, 321 are British. France is next, with 51 rowers.

Of those 519 people who have rowed an ocean, only 32 of them have gone back for more and crossed a second ocean. As we painstakingly hand-pumped our fresh water and tried to ignore the pain of our salt sores and claw hand we began to appreciate why.

29 The Thieving Dorado

'The robb'd that smiles, steals something from the
thief; He robs himself that spends a bootless grief.'
William Shakespeare, *Othello*

If we were to break any records we knew we would have to
lighten the boat, so on Day 36 we had a further clear-out,
chucking ruined provisions and clothes overboard and
pumping out the water which had flooded into the hatches.
During this clear-out one of the more extraordinary incidents
of the trip occurred.

Ben was pumping out one of the hatches, with the handheld
bilge pump, draping the hose over the side so the water flowed
back into the sea. Without any warning a large dorado
appeared from beneath us and snatched the hose in its mouth,
swimming down fast with it. 'You thieving bastard!' Ben
shouted as it snapped the hose from the pump and disappeared, no doubt carrying it off as some sort of exotic gift
for a potential mate. Thereafter we would pump any flooded
water into a bucket, cursing the dorado all the while.

30 Small Aliens from the Deep

'Yea, slimy things did crawl with legs / upon the slimy sea.'
Samuel Taylor Coleridge, *The Rime of
the Ancient Mariner*

That night was the blackest yet with not a star or a slice of
moon to light our way. With no distractions from above I
watched the bioluminescence flare up in the water as the oars
scooped flashes of green, silver and gold. As we passed through
thick patches of bioluminescence, the drops of water falling
from the oars would light up little splashes of gold back on the
surface of the water. In the dark they lit up like shimmering
trails of molten lava.

Other times flecks of luminous green would get stuck on
the oar blade or would creep in through one of the scuppers
to gall brightly on deck. There would be occasional explosions
of colour in the water, no doubt as a larger creature swam
through the clouds of minuscule plankton which flash electric
colours in response to being touched.

When we were going fast, the wave created by our bow
would light up the black sea in streams of gold while, if you
looked out of the back cabin, you could see the rudder wake
creating the same fire-flashes in the water.

I knew that this natural light show came from tiny
zooplankton, but such was our fascination with the beauty of
the displays that we decided to take a look into the gloom
of the night sea to see what we could with a torch. We were

greeted with a horrifying sight. The sea seemed to writhe with millions of pale, minuscule, alien-like creatures fighting their way to escape the beam of light cutting into the abyssal black of their universe.

'Weird,' I said, sweeping the beam across the surface as the zooplankton cowered away from the light.

'That's disgusting. Remind me not to fall in at night,' replied Ben.

It was strange to think that these, the smallest of the sea's creatures, are the foundation of the oceanic food chain and are the diet of the blue whale, the biggest animal ever to have existed.

The word plankton comes from the Greek *planktos* meaning 'drifter' or 'wanderer'. Near the surface live the phytoplanktons, which are plant-like plankton. They live between the surface and a depth of 200 metres, in an area called the epipelagic zone where there is enough sun for them to photosynthesise. Then there is a huge variety of zooplankton, which includes fish larvae, arrow worms, copepods and tiny crustaceans that tend to inhabit the darker mesopelagic zone from 200 to 1,000 metres . . . at least until night. When it gets dark, many of these creatures rise in order to feed on phytoplankton and also each other. Since they spend their lives in the dark, many of these zooplankton are bioluminescent, as are other larger creatures such as the squid which also inhabit the mesopelagic zone and deeper.

It was unnerving to think that on dark, moonless nights, right underneath our barnacled hull there was an almighty struggle for survival going on at a microscopic level. The fact that the zooplankton were so many and varied and that they drifted or propelled themselves through the dark made them seem even more alien, blind in the blackness of space. As the first creatures to have appeared out of the primordial soup around 600 million years ago they are, to my mind, still the strangest that live today.

31 The One Thousand Mile Mark

'The true peace of God begins at any point one thousand miles from the nearest land.'

Joseph Conrad

On Day 37 we rowed past the one thousand miles from Australia mark. Just over a month before we'd never been out of sight of land and now we were one thousand miles from the nearest landfall. My sister sent me the Joseph Conrad quote on our satellite phone, and how apt it was. We had now settled into the routine of life at sea.

All around us was the immensity of the sea and sky. Never for one second was I bored. Instead, while rowing, I was lulled into a hypnotic trance, watching the movement of the sea and the change of the weather overhead. Perhaps it was an illusion, but the sea always appeared to change with our geographical location. The valley of waves through which we travelled so fast after the vortex had given way to a plateau of water that seemed to slope gently, so that every evening it felt like we were rowing slowly downriver. After the utter still of the first becalming we would occasionally go through what we called *Inception* seas, after the mind-bending film, *Inception*. Here it seemed as if the vast sea was being slopped around like the water in a washing-up bowl as it's carried slowly across a room. Long, low walls of water seemed to collide gently with each other from every direction, mixing imperceptibly. There was always something to look at and the vast expanse of water created a peace of mind impossible to find amid the madding crowds on dry land.

We were relentlessly positive. If something broke, which it nearly always did, we were bullish about being able to fix it or find a way around it. We'd come up with little tricks to get around our problems with seeing the compass or using the foot steering; after all, we had plenty of time to think up and try out solutions.

There was the physical pain, but it was easily worth it to be in amid the beauty and solitude of the sea. Also, there was our habit of turning everything into a joke and making fun of each other, which always lightened the mood and prevented us from falling into navel-gazing and misery. Despite some hardships and a few scares, we were having fun. Every Monday morning we would remind ourselves that we weren't in 'the office'. No, now we had a new office, the ocean, and it was one that I felt suited me more than any other workplace I'd been in. Of course, in this new office there were some serious health and safety risks and the pay was non-existent; in fact, I'd given up my lifesavings and more to be there, but it was better than I'd ever hoped for. *No amount of money*, I thought to myself, *would stop us or buy us out of this experience.*

32 The Great Becalming

'The secrets of the currents in the seas have never yet been divulged.'

Herman Melville, *Moby Dick*

For the next 16 days we experienced what we'd later call the great becalming. During this period we averaged only 17 miles a day. By way of comparison, we had averaged 27 miles a day for the previous 16 days and would average 32 miles a day for the 16 days after the great becalming.

What we discovered was that when the wind dropped we were entirely subject to the ocean's currents, and the Indian Ocean is notorious for its fickle, ever-changing currents.

On Day 38 we had headwinds; 15 knots of south-westerly winds were pushing us backwards, so we had to put in the parachute anchor. We lay in the cabin eating neat peanut butter and honey and talking ourselves into eating some of our chocolate supplies. The great becalming would be very bad for our small supply of food luxuries.

I went over the side to clean the hull and was amazed by how quickly the marine growth had returned. Ben had decided that swimming was making his salt sores worse, so he didn't swim much, but I was still keen and loved putting on the mask and seeing what fish I could spot.

We had a metal scraper, which I ran over the hull to remove the barnacles that sat with their arms fanned out in the water catching phytoplankton. As they started their slow, twirling descent into the blue the pilot fish would dart among them, accompanying them down but never seeming to eat them.

The pilot fish, I noticed, were breeding. They massed around our hull, one moment hiding behind the rudder, the next swimming confidently up to my mask to investigate me. We had about twenty of these zebra-striped scavengers who were obviously thriving on the scraps of dinner and buckets of poo that went overboard. As well as the pilots, we also had a cleaner wrasse or 'sucker fish' attached to the hull. Clearly he thought we were some sort of slow-moving whale. We also, to my amazement, had a tiny pale crab that seemed to be busily harvesting the barnacles. How has he clung on through all the rough weather? I wondered. Later on, on Day 50, this little guy scuttled through the scuppers and sat on deck staring at us grumpily. I offered him a minuscule bit of beef jerky, which he immediately ate and seemed to enjoy. It must be one of the strangest inter-species meetings: a crab being fed dried South American beef by a human being in the middle of the Indian Ocean. We never saw him again but occasionally, when we passed floating debris, we would see one of the same species of pale little crabs bossily commandeering the piece of oceanic litter.

We had a shortwave radio and after my swim we managed, for the first time, to pick up the BBC World Service in among the many Chinese stations and the occasional crackly call to prayer. Even though we were going slowly backwards it was a surreal treat to listen to the modulated, reassuring tones of the BBC.

When we brought in the para anchor we noticed that it had attracted a new dorado, more colourful than the others, who seemed to have a harem of duller green females following him. Or maybe it was the other way around; maybe the dull green males were vying for the affections of this

rainbow-coloured female. Maybe she had been the lucky recip-
ient of our hand-pump hose. Either way, I wanted to capture
this new character on film. I stopped coiling the retrieval line
and picked up the camera, plunging it over the side.

'If you pull the main line and inflate the anchor just next
to the boat I think that could be a really good shot with all
the dorados swimming around it,' I said excitedly.

Ben looked at me, bemused: we had just gone six miles
backwards and now I was asking him to delay longer and take
the strain of the para anchor line while I got what I thought
was a good camera shot. Well, it would have been, but it
annoyed him nonetheless and fair enough, but now the multi-
coloured dorado was swimming right up to the camera and
leaping out of the water in a captivating display of gymnastics.
I felt like *I* was being wooed by this magical fish.

'Don't worry about it, *I'll* bring in the para anchor,' said
Ben, frustrated at my distraction.

One of our differences was our attitude to filming. I was
intent, perhaps slightly obsessive, about capturing everything
on film. It's difficult to film nature and it's often the last thing
you want to do when you're tired, but I thought it would be
a better record than the illegible scrawl in my journal. Also,
I felt I owed it to my friend Adam, a producer who wanted
to make a film about the row, to get some decent footage. I've
always loved documentaries and had various ideas about how
our film could be different. Ben would watch me, slightly
perplexed. He did a bit of filming, but I think I appeared to
him like one of those tourists who, always looking through
the lens, misses the 'real' experience.

33 Gyres

'Down dropped the breeze, the sails dropped down,
'Twas sad as sad could be;
And we did speak only to break
The silence of the sea!'

Samuel Taylor Coleridge, *The Rime of
the Ancient Mariner*

Although the going was slow it was beautiful. It tended to be
very sunny at this time, and we were treated to some extraordinary
clouds. One day all the clouds were shaped like pillars,
vast columns of white hanging utterly motionless in the sky.
Another day they were all sitting at exactly the same height,
puffy on top but perfectly flat underneath as if someone had
run a knife along their underside.

It became clear during the great becalming that Ben liked
going fast whereas I preferred to go slow. Ben didn't mind
the dampness that built up in the cabin when we were going
fast and thought speed was more fun than the slower pace
of life in the doldrums. He maintained he wasn't set on
breaking any records, but he was keen to make good time
and would always be working out our average mileage and
likely dates for crossing the halfway point, finishing, and
whatever else. Apart from being too bad at maths to do this,
I honestly didn't care. I thought we'd get there when we got
there and there was no point analysing it. The surfing conditions
could be fun, but I preferred the flat calm during which
I could sleep in a dry cabin, sit on a dry deck and fanny

about with the camera at my leisure. While Ben got frustrated with the calm I got more upset when, on Day 39, one of the two cameras followed the first of our iPods, dying without explanation.

Little or no wind meant we were vulnerable to the strong currents of the Indian Ocean. Sometimes we'd fire along for a couple of hours at three knots only to then come to a halt and barely reach half a knot, even if we rowed together. Rowing together wasn't sustainable, though, so where teams of four can use their greater strength to increase the boat's speed and row with ease through adverse currents we, taking it in turns to row alone, were much more at the currents' mercy.

To make matters worse, we occasionally got stuck in giant circular currents called gyres. These are huge whirlpools in the middle of the ocean where, over time, rubbish collects. We'd realise we were in one because we'd suddenly spot plastic bags and other detritus in the water. It was terrible seeing the pilot fish swallowing tiny bits of plastic and, having grown to think of the ocean as pristine, it was shocking to see so much rubbish.*

Despite the rubbish, these gyres and countercurrents were difficult to detect without looking at our GPS to see what speed we were doing. I came a cropper one morning when the sun was beating down on a blue sea that undulated calmly beneath a cloudless sky. As I rowed, the little swirls of wake created by the oars disappeared much faster than usual, which I thought meant we must be moving through the water at speed. I looked down into the water and saw the pilot fish

---

* The UN Environment Programme estimates that there are up to 13,000 pieces of plastic litter, including 'micro-plastics' smaller than 5mm, in every square kilometre of sea. The problem is worse in the North Pacific Gyre.

swimming hard to keep up with us, jostling playfully for position at the bow of the boat. They seemed to be enjoying
themselves and, looking again at how fast the oar wakes were
vanishing, I realised that I too was enjoying myself. We were
flying along and I was only at the start of my shift. At this
rate I'd be able to clock up some impressive miles by the time
Ben emerged for his turn in four hours. I decided to keep
those miles a surprise so I didn't get up to look at the GPS,
which in the brilliant sun was impossible to read from afar.
Four hours later when Ben came out he looked at the GPS
and said matter-of-factly, 'Ah, so we're going backwards again,
are we?' The current moving against us was so fast that all I
had been doing was keeping the boat in a straight line and
limiting the damage while the water flooded past, dragging
us backwards as the pilot fish swam tirelessly into the current.

34 Sea Stars

'Disturb us, Lord, to dare more boldly,
To venture on wilder seas
Where storms will show Your mastery;
Where losing sight of land,
We shall find the stars.'

From 'The Prayer of
Sir Francis Drake', 1577

While nights could be the toughest of times, with dark fearful storms or eerie lightning in the distance, the calm cloudless ones were the best part of the voyage. It was always unsettling to stare into the pale eternal blue of the afternoon sky and know that it was hiding the dizzy stars. It was never long, though, before they were visible again. We spent as much time awake at night as in the daytime, becoming as familiar with the stars as with the sunshine. On dry land you might go out star gazing one summer's night or you might stay up late indoors, but very rarely are you awake, active and outside during the night on a regular basis.

With half of our time spent awake during the darkness we felt ourselves becoming creatures of the night. Our night vision would improve dramatically after the first twenty minutes of the shift and, with no light pollution to interfere, I was able to see more stars than I'd ever seen or imagined was possible.

On starry, moonless nights we were treated to incredible displays of shooting stars. They were so regular that I stopped recording even the most impressive ones in my journal. Before then, I would note down how long their fiery wake would burn its trail across the sky; often four or five seconds.

Even more impressive was the phenomenon we called 'exploding stars'. These were the larger meteors which, on entering our atmosphere, seemed to explode in a flash of distant light that reminded me of grainy footage of night bombing. It was very apparent on these clear nights that we are under a constant bombardment from outer space. I reported one particularly bright and low-falling star because it burnt orange like a flare and seemed to touch down in the sea. Tony said he'd informed the Australian coastguard of a similar sight in 2009, and they had replied that it was probably 'space junk', an old satellite re-entering the atmosphere and burning up.

We were over one thousand miles from Australia and hadn't seen any ships or planes for weeks. Could the falling star have been a meteor that was big enough to get through the atmosphere? Hundreds of small ones do get through, as do larger ones such as the 1908 Tunguska impact in which an asteroid levelled 80 million trees in a remote Siberian forest. While asteroids have intermittently wreaked havoc on Earth for most of its history and probably wiped out the dinosaurs 65 million years ago, some scientists argue that they brought life to earth in the first place. We are all made of stardust, as they say. But even a relatively small meteor hitting the ocean would cause a massive tsunami, and I wondered how we'd fare in our rowing boat.

Behind the array of shooting stars were the real stars, moving slowly through the sky and flickering like distant flames. I recognised constellations such as the Southern Cross, with its two pointer stars, shining reassuringly as it climbed towards the horizon and finally disappeared in the early hours. Then there were other formations of stars that I used to get my bearing, but whose names I didn't know. With some stars so much brighter than others there was a depth to the sky that meant I felt I could see which were nearer and which more distant. This gave a sense of perspective, as if I could perceive our place in space.

But dwarfing these petty constellations was the Milky Way in all its mad glory. Curving its way across my right shoulder from the horizon in front to the horizon behind, its density made the rest of the patchy stars look almost desolate. On calm nights the stars would be reflected back off the flat, black sea into the gold-flecked darkness of the sky above. This heightened the impression I often got, floating on the ocean at night, that we were nothing but a minuscule piece of flotsam or perhaps plankton drifting through space itself. I say it was an impression, but of course it's true. We were on one ocean of our planet, orbiting our sun, which itself is one medium-sized star halfway along one arm of one particular pin-wheel galaxy. When we look at the Milky Way we are looking at the dense centre of this, our galaxy. The Hubble Space Telescope has observed 3,000 galaxies, although NASA's estimate puts the total number of galaxies at 125 billion. There are those nights when you sit at home, eating dinner, watching telly, thinking about the trivial battles that make up day-to-day existence, but during those nights on the ocean I genuinely felt like an astronaut who had been cast off into the eternity of space. It's little wonder that, as I lay in the cabin of our isolated boat, gazing out the back hatch at the wheeling stars, I would often say to myself, as the alarm for my shift sounded, 'Is there really any point bothering to row?' At which point the cabin door would open and Ben would say, 'Your go.'

35 'If'

'If you can dream – and not make dreams your master.'

Rudyard Kipling, 'If'

By the time we'd been at sea for six weeks not only had land become a distant memory but the very idea of it seemed strange. The only smell was the salty air which, while refreshing, could also be monotonous. The salty spray was relentless in its corrosion, rusting everything it could and breaking down our very skin. Our boat had a copper-bottomed hull to avoid attracting too much marine growth and we occasionally joked that we should have coppered our own bottoms, such was their continual disintegration. The sea is a harsh environment and sometimes the ideas of land, of people, of the softness of a woman, became almost abstract in their strangeness. I thought a lot about Tory. I had a bundle of letters from her, with one to open every fortnight. After a month at sea I started to measure out the days according to how long I had until I could open the next one. We used the satellite phone, too, to make contact with girlfriends, family or friends once every week or so. Their reactions were often quite funny. We called a friend once when he was in Paddington station. All he could say for the first few minutes was, 'I'm in Paddington, I'm actually in Paddington,' and then to someone behind him in the ticket queue, 'Middle of the Indian Ocean.'

These brief conversations always lifted our spirits, but life still revolved around our 23-foot-long floating world. Towards the end of the great becalming our watermaker packed in again. We went through the same psychological loop; at first getting increasingly frustrated at our failed attempts to fix it, but later cheering up as we got out the hand pump and started spending more time on deck.

We came up with games for keeping ourselves entertained. We learnt the poem 'If' by heart, then timed ourselves to see who could say it the fastest, or did alternate lines, words and syllables before finally trying to say it backwards and discovering we weren't that desperate. We played actor tennis, in which one person names an actor and a film they were in to which the other person replies with another actor who was in that film and a film they were in. The problem with this game was, having lived in a container in the Sudan for many years, Ben's knowledge of 21st-century cinema was limited and he tried to bring everything back to *Armageddon*. It was easy to ace him, as I did with Morgan Freeman narrating *March of the Penguins*.

36 Whale!

'There she blows! There! There! She blows! She blows!'
Herman Melville, *Moby Dick*

I had to wait until Day 46 to shout, 'There she blows!', but it was worth it. Even though we hadn't yet started reading *Moby Dick*, whales have always loomed large in my imagination and the prospect of encountering any was hugely exciting. We had up until this point only heard whales blowing at night and had caught snippets of what we thought might be sonar whilst lying in the cabin, but we'd had no clear sightings.

Then on Day 46, while rowing under a puffy tunnel of clouds, a whale breached barely thirty metres from us. Its sleek, black back arched out of the water as it shot a tall spume of spray from its blowhole. I shouted and Ben was out of the cabin in an instant. Then, as I fumbled for the camera, it breached again, closer this time, showing a tiny dorsal fin on its long back as it cruised past with effortless speed.

We were elated; the sight of the whale made all the pain and work worthwhile. The next day we saw another and this time it swam right underneath the boat but too quickly for us to get a picture and by the time we jumped in it had gone. It looked like a finback, but at the latitudes we were in it is possible it was one of the finback's two close cousins; the Bryde's and the Sei whales.

The finback whale is big; it is the second largest animal on the planet after the blue whale, but its most striking feature is its speed. It can sustain speeds of just over 20 knots. This made it relatively safe from the whalers in the days of *Moby Dick* who would give chase in open rowing boats. As Melville writes:

> The Fin Back is not gregarious. He seems a whale-hater, as some men are man-haters. Very shy; always going solitary; unexpectedly rising to the surface in the remotest and most sullen waters; his straight and single lofty jet rising like a tall misanthropic spear upon a barren plane; gifted with such wondrous power and velocity in swimming, as to defy all present pursuit from man; this leviathan seems to be the banished and unconquerable Cain of his race, bearing for his mark that style upon his back.

We would see more whales again later, but this first encounter was mesmerising. Suddenly it really did feel like we were sharing a home with these noble creatures.

Finback whales can live up to 140 years, although that doesn't make them the most long-lived of the cetaceans. Recent tests have put one bowhead whale's age at 211 years. By far the most amazing fact about whales was that they chose to go back in. The fossil record shows that, having evolved from sea creatures into land animals, akin to squat hippos, whales then went back into the sea to become the majestic circumnavigators we know so little about. This process happened over millions of years, but they still have vestiges of the hands and feet they used on land and, despite diving to unfathomable depths to hunt the primordial squid or braving the severe temperatures of the poles, whales haven't yet evolved gills so still come up to breathe, just like us. In fact, their closest genetic relatives are mice. It seems that by deciding to go back into the sea whales have chosen the freedom of the boundless ocean, just as we had done. Perhaps this is a fanciful idea, but it appealed to us.

37 Our Birds

'I have the feeling of having known my birds forever,
of being here forever without time passing.'
Bernard Moitessier, *The Long Way*

On Day 52, as we were struggling through another day of slow
water, a bird appeared which we had never seen before. Ben
was rowing and I was sitting on the gunwale pumping water
when out of nowhere a white bird with a long tail appeared.
It hovered just above Ben's head, eyeing him quizzically. It
was a white-tailed tropicbird. These birds lay their eggs on
land and then spend the rest of their lives out at sea, feeding
on small fish and squid. We would see a few more during the
trip, and they always seemed surprised to bump into us during
their oceanic wanderings.

The plainer-looking shearwaters were with us every single
day. They get their name from the 'shearing' technique they use
to fly between the waves without ever flapping their wings.
Every day we'd see them gliding in and out of the waves, banking
steeply in front of us and disappearing within seconds on the
strong gusts of wind. We rarely saw the shearwaters flap their
wings and only ever spotted them sitting on the water once.
On this occasion they sat bobbing incongruously like the most
pedestrian of ducks, as if they'd suddenly become bored of
their aerial acrobatics. The rest of the time they flew effortlessly
by, never getting wet and never seeming to dip their beaks in
the water as the storm petrels did, only flying and watching.

At the beginning of our voyage we kept thinking that any day soon we'd lose sight of the shearwaters but every day they were there, swooping near us, dipping their rigid little wings as they rode the thermals. Every day, without fail, they would come and say hello, sociably circling or playfully dive-bombing us. We didn't see a plane from the end of the first week to the last day, so the skies belonged to the shearwaters alone.

38 Shark!

'The un-harming sharks, they glided by as if with
padlocks on their mouths.'
                              Herman Melville, *Moby Dick*

On Day 53 we were rowing uncomfortably on a beam sea with
southerly winds shoving along the waves, which continually
hit us from the side. It was in these choppy waves that I saw
a blue shark. At first it was a shadow, but as it turned towards
the boat its powerful, blue body glimmered in the sunlight.
It circled us. With each swim-by we could see its cold black
eyes scanning the boat and looking up through the surface at
us. It was about eight feet long. Could he jump out of the
water and take one of us? I wondered, having often daydreamed
about the physics of such an attack. On the shark's white
underbelly I spotted the streaming form of a cleaner wrasse,
attached to its host near the concealed jaws.

There was something deeply disturbing in the constant
movement of the shark. It was powerful and lethargic at the
same time. I'd learnt that sharks have evolved differently from
most fish. The majority of fish have a swim bladder, a sort
of in-built buoyancy system. But sharks, lacking the swim
bladder, have to keep swimming all the time otherwise they
will slowly sink to the bottom. Sharks are one of the oldest
species on earth; they were swimming in this lazily murderous
way over 350 million years ago, a good 100 million years
before the first dinosaurs. That's not to say they haven't

evolved since then, but there remains something ancient and amoral about them. To have survived and prospered for so long they have had to be efficient, versatile predators.

The blue shark is thought to be the fastest swimmer of all sharks and it is found in all three major oceans. The few sharks that have been tagged and monitored by scientists have recorded swims of thousands of miles, often across oceans.

Sharks' image as pelagic wanderers seemed appropriate when we met our blue in the middle of the ocean. It didn't stop moving; swimming in its continual eel-like motion around the boat in wide, watchful circles. *No wonder they don't last long in aquariums*, I thought, *they need all the space in the world no less.* I'd read how, when put in an aquarium, a blue shark will only last a month before dying. The longest one has lived for in captivity is seven months, before the shark's mysterious death. In this regard they remind me of terrible stories of Native American Indians who, having lived a lifetime of freedom on the boundless midwestern plains, died within a few days if they were captured and imprisoned.

I watched the shark for some time before I decided to try and film him. I ducked into the cabin and looked out the camera, but by the time I resurfaced he was gone, disappeared into the veiled waters of the ocean.

39 Drier than Being Dry

'We felt very nice and snug, the more so since it was so chilly out of doors ... because truly to enjoy bodily warmth, some small part of you must be cold, for there is no quality in this world that is not what it is merely by contrast. If you flatter yourself that you are all over comfortable, and have been so for a long time, then you cannot be said to be comfortable any more.

'But if, like Queequeg and me in bed, the tip of your nose or the crown of your head be slightly chilled, why then, indeed, in the general consciousness you feel most delightfully and unmistakably warm. For this reason a sleeping apartment should never be furnished with a fire, which is one of the luxurious discomforts of the rich.'

Herman Melville, *Moby Dick*

On Day 54 the wind was 'clocking', which means the wind direction slowly moves around in a circle before settling in the more favourable south-easterly direction, which in the Indian Ocean constitutes what mariners call the trade winds. With the wind against us in its sweep of the clock we were in the cabin, playing magnetic Scrabble. Having lost at magnetic chess, Ben would now only play Scrabble. He doesn't like to lose and had won the first two games of the trip, but here in the third instalment I was about to go massively into the lead. As I announced my word and was halfway through describing how I would cash in on both a triple letter and a double word score, Ben said, 'Wait, can you feel it changing?'

The weather was beginning to come from behind; small waves were tapping at the stern and every so often we could hear a brief whoosh as we moved forwards through the water.

'Okay, let's finish this first and then get rowing.'

'No way, this is our chance to do some miles.'

'You're only saying that because you're losing at Scrabble for the first time; now I've remembered the rules you're running scared.'

But he couldn't be persuaded and, gifting me the game, he started rowing for our best run of the trip. Over the next three days we covered 160 miles. We'd managed roughly the same distance in the last ten days.

It was good to be on the go again, surfing down waves and counting down the miles in each shift. There were some big waves out there and it always took a while for all the waves to get behind us. Even after a day of wind and swell coming from one direction there would still be rogue waves that cut across the rest. We invented acronyms to describe them. The small ones which slapped the side of the boat and leapt up, splashing us insultingly in the eyes were called Angry Port Side waves (APS) or Angry Starboard Side waves (ASS). The big ones that rocked the boat over, filled her up or spun her round were called Monumental Angry Port Side waves (MAPS), and so on. Not being true sailors and retaining our suspicion of the related terminology, we made up our own acronyms for nearly everything. The radio antennae were the Sock Drying Poles (SDPs). Ben would still tell me off whenever I used nautical language. 'What's a lanyard?' he'd say in all seriousness. 'All I can see is a bit of rope.' We even ended up calling the oars 'the wooden planks' or 'the long things'.

The big weather was back and the rowing was fun, but the

cabin once again became damp and uncomfortable. On entering the cabin for a sleep we would struggle out of our foul-weather gear, normally getting thrown against the sides of the cabin when half undressed. Then, lying down, the cycling shorts came off and various lotions and potions were applied to the bottom.

At this stage in the trip we started hugging our cycling shorts to our chests, which dried them out over the few hours of rest. Weirdly, it was nice to feel a little bit of damp close to my body as I lay wrapped up in the camping quilt, which nearly always managed to remain dry. Those damp cycling shorts, held close, reminded me of what I wasn't doing and made me feel drier than being totally dry could ever feel.

It is truly all in the contrasts. While I've never worked as hard physically as rowing twelve hours a day, I've never felt as rested as after occasional nights in the cabin when we slept for as much as eight hours. A tin of tuna has never tasted, nor will ever taste, as good as the one we had at our halfway party. Deprivation and difficulty only served to heighten any small moments of comfort, so that snatches of relief often seemed almost absurdly ecstatic.

40 The Moon

> 'Moreover, if you accept the ordinary laws of science, you have to suppose that human life and life in general on this planet will die out in due course: it is a stage in the decay of the solar system; at a certain stage of decay you get the sort of conditions of temperature and so forth which are suitable to protoplasm, and there is life for a short time in the life of the whole solar system. You see in the moon the sort of thing to which the earth is tending – something dead, cold, and lifeless.'
>
> Bertrand Russell, 'Why I Am Not a Christian'

The full moon at this time was sometimes so bright the night would feel more like daylight. In the rough, following seas that brought us so many miles we were able to see the waves, anticipate them and line the boat up to get the most out of them. When the moon was behind us a long runway of glistening, liquid silver stretched out over the water as we sped along.

We'd worked out that if we successfully rowed across the Indian Ocean we would cover the same distance as halfway across the surface of the moon. Looking up at the cratered surface of the moon, which appeared freakishly close, made this a tiring thought.

Although its brightness blotted out the stars the moon was mesmerising in itself. How strange to think that, according to the giant impact theory, the cold moon was once part of our planet, formed when Earth collided with the planet Theia, sending a large number of moonlets into orbit. These moonlets eventually joined together to form the moon. It was this impact that tilted our planet on its side and gave rise to the very specific conditions that made life on earth possible.

We couldn't help but feel a connection with the moon, and its gravitational pull that governs the tides. By now, we knew when it would rain, where the moon would come up and how much of it we would be able to see. It was therefore a surprise when it disappeared before my eyes on Day 56.

I was rowing along in the dead of night, with the moon behind my back illuminating the bulkhead in front of me in its luminous blue light. Then all of a sudden it started to dim and, turning around, I saw the edge of the moon blackening. I stopped rowing, scrambled over the deck and opened the cabin door.

'Wake up; I think there's a lunar eclipse!' I said excitedly.

'Leave me alone, I'm sleeping.'

Fair enough, I thought. *Maybe I'm seeing things.*

But over the next twenty minutes the moon disappeared as the earth cast more of its shadow across its surface. Watching it gradually darken really intensified that feeling of moving through space. Eventually there was a halo of dull light glowing around the black sphere and the stars once again flickered all around. There I sat watching the blackened moon from the black sea until the process started reversing itself and the moon's blue light crept back over the water.

The next day I switched on the satellite phone and the first text to come through read, 'Did you manage to see the lunar eclipse last night?'

41 Halfway Point in the Sea of Rainbows

'Alone, alone, all, all alone,
Alone on a wide wide sea!'
Samuel Taylor Coleridge,
The Rime of the Ancient Mariner

On Day 59 we passed the halfway point. We had been experiencing biblical rainfall all the previous day and night and still showers were passing overhead. But the sun was there in the gaps so that rainbows beamed in every direction. Full rainbows, half rainbows, double rainbows; they were everywhere and they were close. It was possible to see their ends dipping into clouds or looping into the water.

In this sea of rainbows we crossed the halfway point and shook hands. Every mile now was one mile closer to Mauritius. Apart from, of course, when we were going backwards, which we didn't doubt we would be doing again. But here we were in one of the most beautiful and isolated places in the world, halfway to achieving our dream and, as Tony told us, only thirty-four miles behind the record. With the weather still behind us we decided to put off our halfway party for a calm day and carried on rowing as normal.

On Day 62 that calm day came. First, we managed to fix the watermaker by rigging up a header tank. Someone would still have to stay on deck to feed it for a couple of hours each day but it was a lot less work than pumping. Then we made our celebration meal. We'd agreed that there would be no freeze-dried food, so we delved into the small bag of 'land food' we had brought. We made a salad with two tins of tuna, one tin of sweetcorn and one tin of beetroot. A dash of Tabasco, and it made the finest meal I've ever tasted; the rich oiliness of the fish against the sweetness of the vegetables was exquisite. We drank two miniature bottles of champagne to accompany our feast.

There we sat, looking out over the untroubled water, surely two of the most isolated people on the planet. I was so proud of what we had achieved in rowing halfway across the Indian Ocean under our own steam, and we congratulated each other under the fiery sunset.

Finishing the champagne, we found ourselves quite light-headed and decided we were still hungry. Like two foraging bears we riffled out some chocolate and ate it, then drank some of our brandy, smoked some cigarettes and then decided it would be a good idea to eat some more chocolate. It was a surreal feeling, treating ourselves as if we were on a holiday boating trip when we were actually over one and a half thousand miles from the nearest land.

As darkness settled on the calm we stumbled, exhausted, into the cabin where we fell asleep, giddily happy, like two old men who had broken out of their retirement home and spent a night in the local pub.

42 *Moby Dick*

> 'I am half way in the work . . . It will be a strange
> sort of book.'
>
> Herman Melville, on writing *Moby Dick*

It had been hard work getting to the halfway point and, as
we resumed our relentless routine of rowing and sleeping, we
realised that all halfway means is that you've got to do it all
over again. We would need something to keep us going, something to look forward to, and so we decided to start reading
Moby Dick.

It worked. Now every day as we rowed we knew that we
could look forward to another instalment of this massive
tale with its many meandering deviations and musings.
As the story unfolded, we came to see the similarities
between ocean rowing and whaling. When talking about
the characters attracted to whaling in the mid nineteenth
century, and the very business of being at sea for long
periods, Melville could have been talking about the world
of ocean rowing. When the whaling ships caught up with
a sperm whale they would lower rowing boats in which the
crew would give chase, which means that much of the book
is about rowing around in the middle of the ocean in the
shadow of a watery death.

Herman Melville wrote *Moby Dick* in 1851 when he was 31
years old. He had served on one of the many Nantucket
whaling ships that circumnavigated the globe, hunting sperm

whales for their oil. Melville had jumped ship in the South Seas and lived there for two years before returning to America to become a writer. He had some early successes, but *Moby Dick* was a flop and his writing career went on the slide until he took a job at the New York Custom House in 1866, where he worked until his death in 1891.

Moby Dick tells the story of Captain Ahab's obsessive pursuit of a white sperm whale; the eponymous Moby Dick. Ahab sails over the Atlantic and Indian Oceans, enquiring of each whale ship he meets, 'Hast ye seen the white whale?', until he eventually tracks Moby Dick down in the Pacific.

Using the narrative of Ahab's obsessive quest as his backdrop, Melville exhaustively describes every aspect of whaling, whales and life at sea. With all the time in the world on our hands we were constantly entertained by his many factual and metaphysical digressions. Even when Melville occasionally gets his facts wrong, like assuming from the available evidence that the whale is surely a fish and not a mammal, he writes captivatingly about the wild beauty and unforgiving danger of the ocean.

One of us would sit in the cabin with the hatch open, reading aloud to the rower, shouting or singing when required, stopping only to sip sweet tea or to argue a point.

Perhaps it was because we came to love the book so much that we saw so many comparisons between whaling and ocean rowing. As I've said, I related to Ahab's injury-driven obsession (if not its object), and there were many other comparisons to draw too. Nobody ever got rich rowing an ocean and likewise the crews of whaling ships served on long two- or three-year voyages for negligible returns. They were in it for the adventure and to escape the mundanity of landlubbing, just as we were. Obviously, we didn't want to slaughter whales to the point of extinction, but *Moby Dick* is about so much more than just whaling and it became as much as a comfort to us as a Bible might be for a God-fearing seaman.

On inspecting the boat at Gallions Reach we took the seller's word that she floated. Still my head swum with questions, foremost of which was, 'Will Ben really insist on bringing the mustard coloured cords?'

Fixing up the boat. What we lacked in knowledge (and we lacked a lot) we made up for in enthusiasm, although we spent a fair amount of time surreptitiously gluing things to each other.

We put the names of everyone who sponsored us on the boat and whilst at sea spent many hours telling stories which illustrated what we liked about each person.

At the check-out at Heathrow we were naive and clean shaven, both of which were soon to change.

Preparing to launch the boat at Geraldton with no time to make any more changes. Fully laden she weighed over a tonne.

Leaving Geraldton at dawn on Day 1 it took us quite a while to navigate out of the marina, so onlookers could easily have been forgiven for wondering if we'd ever find our way across the Indian Ocean.

On our way, Paddington lashed to the prow like some latter-day Odysseus, Ben is feeding the watermaker having just put his socks to dry on the radio antennae – better known as the SDPs or Sock Drying Poles.

We only rowed together on a few rare occasions when we tried to counter the countercurrents.

owing west we had the rising sun on our face and the setting sun on our backs every day.

No one day ever looked the same during the voyage.

Rowing as a pair, you spend most of your time alone with your thoughts as the other person sleeps.

Sometimes our chats in between shifts lasted longer than they should as we took to arguing about films, Celine Dion and navigation.

Surf's Up! Hand-steering the boat as she surfed the waves we started to wonder if we could do the whole voyage like this. Sadly it turned out we had to row.

Ben displays one of our biggest catches of the trip: a tiny flying fish who threw himself into the boat.

Part of our philosophy was that, while not always knowing what we were doing, we should at least try to look the part. Ben had his own unique interpretation of this philosophy.

Most evenings we would collect and steel ourselves with some grog and a cigarette before going into the night shifts.

One of the eerie calms we encountered in which nothing broke the surface of the sea except our oars... and sometimes not even those.

Each day the sun appeared and disappeared and we saw it every time.

Ben getting ready to document the first swim, which took place on Day 17 in water 5,000 metres deep.

In one of the weirder episodes of the trip, Timothy the moth lands and stays the night with us, over 700 nautical miles from land.

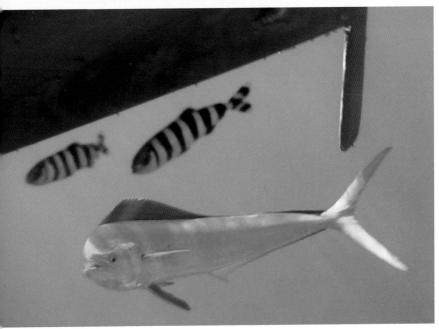

Some of our constant companions: the pilot fish and one of the dorados.

Swimming around the boat to take this photo, I was struck by how impossibly small she appeared.

Ben called this 'sunning the bottom' and it formed part of his quite unconventional stretching routine. Whilst no doubt necessary it could be a disturbing sight to wake up to.

Ben checking his watch five minutes into a rough, rainy shift and realising that he still has another two hours and fifty five minutes to go. No photo sums up the reality of ocean rowing better.

Pumping for water by hand was hard work but it was good to spend time together on deck.

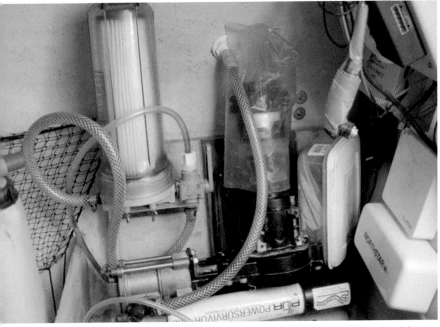

The watermaker. No point pretending this ever served us well as it gave us trouble from the first week to the last, but we were always grateful for any water it made us.

The cabin and the star-gazing hatch. Without doubt the most comfortable place to be on board, apart from when it was wet or when we were forced to top and tail during stormy nights.

We were surprised by how cold the first 1,000 miles were and often found ourselves wearing our foul weather gear to stay warm.

Leaving the rescue boat with Ben's dad we were seconds away from stepping onto dry land for the first time in four months.

I'd dreamed of being re-united with Tory during the row but hadn't thought I'd have to swim the last bit to get there.

Celebrating with our French Mauritian rescuers.

Back on *terra firma* in Mauritius and struggling to blend in with the other honeymooners.

43 Passing Ships

> 'Some merchant ships crossing each other's wake in
> the mid-Atlantic, will oftentimes pass on without
> so much as a single word of recognition, mutually
> cutting each other on the high seas, like a brace of
> dandies in Broadway.'
>
> Herman Melville, *Moby Dick*

The evening of Day 63 was dark. It was a night so black, with
not a star or hint of moon behind the low clouds, that we
decided to turn on the navigation light. This small light at
the front of the boat cast an eerie shadow over the surrounding
sea and all night we could see the pale flashes of the ghost-like
dorado as they sped under the hull in pursuit of their prey.
Rowing the first night shift I nearly turned off the navigation
light, thinking I'd prefer the pitch black to a dim glow that
barely illuminated the boat.

All of a sudden there was a great commotion behind me.
A thrashing and splashing, but as I turned around all I could
see was a large patch of white water. Had a whale sounded as
quickly as it had breached? Had a shark taken one of the
dorado? Or was it something else? This was the problem with
rowing, you always had your back turned to your direction
of travel. Despite the thousands of miles of open ocean, it
still felt unnatural not to be looking where you were going.

Luckily the GPS sounded an alarm later in the night to
warn us of an oncoming container ship, the motor vessel *CMA*

CGM Blue Whale. It was the first ship we'd seen since Day 11 and as it loomed into sight we excitedly called it up on the VHF radio. We reported our position and the master confirmed that he would give us a wide berth, but he asked nothing of who we were or what we were doing. Clearly we were just a dot on their computer system that needed to be avoided.

'They're just like bus drivers,' Ben said disparagingly.

'*Blue Whale,* hast ye seen the white whale?' I joked, paraphrasing Captain Ahab, but already the ship was pulling away to the east, its lights fading as it disappeared with its towering stacks of containers.

44 Splendid Isolation

'This most excellent canopy,
the air, look you, this brave o'erhanging firmament,
this majestical roof fretted with golden fire.'
William Shakespeare, *Hamlet*

No matter how dark or difficult the nights, the sun would always rise, heralded at first by the morning stars. The sunrise nearly always appeared like an upbeat, motivational poster, with thick beams of light dappling the ocean, and night would be forgotten as we began to warm up and dry out.

However clichéd, the sun's beauty and warmth were always a relief after those tough nights in which we made little progress and during which we were becoming more tired as we lost weight and became nutritionally deprived.

On the evening of Day 67 the red sun sank below the horizon as the sky was already filling with stars. We had slowed down again and decided to enjoy the night instead of battling away into yet another countercurrent. Watching the GPS for a while, we worked out that if we didn't row for two hours we'd go back only half a mile. It wasn't even a debate. As it was calm and dry we had the iPod on deck and chose a piece of Renaissance choral music called *Spem in alium*. We each leant back onto the bulkhead, one on either side of the deck, passing the whisky and smoking our last few cigarettes.

'We're all in the gutter, but some of us are looking at the stars,' I quoted.

'Oscar Wilde; he had some good ones, didn't he?'

'Yeah, he also had one of the top ten deathbed quotes: "Either that wallpaper goes or I do," which is up there with Spike Milligan's: "I told you I was ill.".'

'Who said, "Punctuality is the virtue of the bored"?'

'Not sure, but if we take an embarrassingly long time getting to Mauritius we can just say we had better things to do than row.'

'Good plan; this is much more fun than rowing.'

We stared up at the flashing satellites as they tracked silently across the immense, star-clouded sky. Of all the amazing nights we had on the ocean this was the best.

But did we talk each other into taking breaks too easily? Even with the relentless rounds of countercurrents should we not have been pushing all the time? Despite our mutual belief that records were relatively meaningless, our morale tended to be higher when we were going fast. So, on Day 72, when we spent the first four hours of the day hurtling along at four knots we were on a high and when later that day we slowed, so did our spirits. Perhaps it was the feeling of rowing hard and going nowhere, of working and achieving nothing, that grated. When it was tough, it was hard to remember that in adverse conditions it was a victory simply to stay stationary.

Having a great experience and getting to Mauritius, these were our common goals, but as the trip wore on it seemed like we weren't having that great experience unless we were making decent progress towards Mauritius. At this time I was experiencing the usual pain, stiffness and sores, but Ben was in agony on account of some serious bowel trouble. The bucket was my friend, but it had now become his enemy. This must have played a part in his newfound focus on the finish line, while I felt more unhurried, sensing that Mauritius meant the end of the adventure. I didn't feel any urgency to get to the finish line. The ocean was beautiful and always interesting and, most importantly, it was turning out to be everything I'd dreamt of when crammed into the underground on a Monday morning. I was lost in my own little world and I had no interest in re-entering what others called the 'real world' any time soon.

45 Reveries

'There you stand, lost in the infinite series of the
sea, with nothing ruffled but the waves. The
tranced ship indolently rolls; the drowsy trade
winds blow; everything resolves you into languor.
For the most part, in this tropic whaling life, a
sublime uneventfulness invests you; you hear no
news; read no gazettes; extras with startling
accounts of commonplaces never delude you into
unnecessary excitements; you hear no domestic
afflictions; bankrupt securities; falls of stocks; are
never troubled with the thought of what you shall
have for dinner – for all your meals for three years
and more are snugly stowed in casks, and your bill
of fare is immutable.'

Herman Melville, *Moby Dick*

We'd been at sea for over two months and I now saw our tiny
floating world as just as real and busy and complex as the
world we'd left behind. At the start of the trip I still felt like
we were missing out; when we heard of Bin Laden's death or
the royal wedding it was as if we were hearing second-hand
of something that we would otherwise have been directly
involved in. This is, of course, the illusion created by rolling
news, air travel, the internet and all the other facets of the
21st-century global village, which combine to make you feel
connected to every celebrity and part of every major event.

But when, a couple of months in, we received a message
telling us that the stock market was crashing again it meant

nothing to us. The only thing that could have roused our interest was news of an approaching hurricane. The rise and fall of banks meant nothing; we only worried about the direction or strength of the wind. In the middle of the vast ocean, under the infinity of the sky, it didn't matter what the FTSE 100 or the housing market was doing, and neither did we have to hear about it. The very solitude was lulling me into a trancelike state.

When you're rowing as a pair you spend nearly all your time alone. When you take over from the other person you share a brief joke, an observation or perhaps some advice. Then, as you sit down in the rowing seat, the cabin door closes, your rowing partner retires and all is silence. Once again you are alone.

I was never bored while rowing. I watched the sea and sky in their constant change or followed the dorado surfing in the wave behind or the shearwaters wheeling in the sky above. The beauty and rhythm of this environment lulled me into meditative thoughts. I would sort through the past, admonishing myself where necessary, but also forgiving myself. The human mind in this situation is prone, though, to obsession and there were subjects and people who kept cropping up, even though I thought I had dealt with them. When there was nothing new to think about or analyse I would ban these subjects from my mind and forbid myself from going over them again. But mainly I would think about the future, planning everything I wanted to do with Tory and how best I could get back on the ocean again, only next time in more comfort. I debated whether or not I should go back to my old job and weighed up my other options. Should I buy that pub in the Scilly Isles, or become a teacher? Sail round the world or fulfil my lifelong ambition of writing a book? I dreamt up children's stories and then pitched them to Ben as he sleepily emerged from the cabin.

'So, there's this octopus right, but he's also an inspector, who investigates underwater mysteries.'

'Okay, what's he called?'

'Inspoctopus.'

'I'm worried about you, mate.'

I also spent a fair amount of time going carefully through each step of what I'd do if I won the Lottery. Occasionally I'd go down more unusual avenues such as hosting an imaginary drinks party for all the bit-part players in my life. I'd wander through the room introducing people I hadn't seen since primary school to obscure clients I'd only ever spoken to on the phone or setting up second cousins with friends' ex-girlfriends.

Did I ever get bored? Never. Did I talk to myself? Absolutely, but then people talk to themselves all the time, the only difference being that on dry land they keep getting interrupted.

46 The Fire Ship

'By midnight the works were in full operation . . .
the wild ocean darkness was intense. But that
darkness was licked up by the fierce flames, which
at intervals forked forth from the sooty flues, and
illuminated every lofty rope in the rigging, as with
the famed Greek fire. The burning ship drove on,
as if remorselessly commissioned to some vengeful
deed.'

Herman Melville, *Moby Dick*

By Day 73 we had a following sea again. Although the wind
was favourable it could be dangerous when it got up to 25
knots and above. The wind would catch the side of the boat
and spin it out onto the beam where it was vulnerable to
oncoming waves.

So, in the night of Day 73, I paused during my first shift
to eat some rice pudding. I'd been looking forward to it for
the previous two hours but when I stopped rowing and opened
the packet the wind pushed us round and we were caught by
a breaking wave. I was completely drenched, the deck swamped
and the packet of rice pudding full to the brim with seawater.
I would have to go hungry and be more careful in future.

Earlier in the day our sailing family friend, Nick Eyles, had
called. We questioned him about countercurrents, trying to
find out if they would persist for the rest of the voyage.
Surprisingly he said, 'There aren't many people who have
spent as long as you have on the Indian Ocean, so you

probably know as well as anyone else.' This should have worried us, because we didn't really have a clue what governed the mercurial currents. Instead I swelled with pride. Yes, very few people had spent this amount of time on the Indian, barely a few feet above the waterline and this must mean that we were very able, possibly very brilliant, seamen. Such was my pride that, in its customary manner, the sea would soon dish up a fall for me.

Before that, though, there was time for some more pride, just to make the fall worse. We had just passed the two thousand miles from Australia mark and were not far from entering our final one thousand miles. We received some generous messages, such as one from Roger Haines saying that we'd come a long way since he had taught us to row at the Skiff Club five months previously. Teddington did indeed seem a long way away.

On Day 74 we were still making good headway and rowed a fifty-mile day in a sea that now seemed to be brimming with life. As large clouds passed overhead a cloud of flying fish, the size of goldfish, leapt out of the water right next to us in flight from a dorado.

That night we were treated to an unholy sight. Out of the murky horizon appeared a ship, *Methane Nile Eagle*. As this ship neared we could see from her superstructure that she was a liquefied natural gas tanker. Instead of the usual navigational lights on the bow, bridge and stern that we had seen on the dry bulk ships, this vessel seemed to be decked in gold light. Passing less than a mile away from us, her demonic bulk, which was nearly 300m long, gleamed. In contrast to the pitch black of the night, she seemed as if from another world. We spoke to the master on the VHF radio. He sounded Greek and, once again, was totally disinterested in us. We were keen for at least a short conversation, but he wasn't playing ball and said, no, he hadn't seen the white whale. Still, we agreed, he was missing out on the real thing. How could you truly experience the ocean from the high, warm bridge of a steel ship doing a steady 14 knots no matter the conditions?

As quickly as it had appeared the ghostly fire ship started to recede back into the darkness. Soon we could only see a flickering light between the waves before she was engulfed in the black night. We were alone, again.

47 The Great Independence Day Wave

'There we sat up to our knees in the sea, the water covering every rib and plank, so that to our downward gazing eyes the suspended craft seemed a coral boat grown up to us as from the bottom of the ocean.'

Herman Melville, *Moby Dick*

I woke up on the morning of Day 75 to find that the wind had picked up so much as to make it virtually impossible to keep the boat lined up with the waves. It had been building through the night and, as I opened the cabin door at dawn, Ben gave a shrug as if to say, 'What can we do in this?'

'It's impossible to stay lined up, I haven't been able to row for the last twenty minutes,' said Ben, who was wrapped up in his waterproofs with his hood zipped up to hide everything but his eyes.

The waves were big but not breaking, so we rose and fell without any splashes. 'I'll make breakfast,' I said.

Over our porridge we discussed what a tough night it had been. The wind was moving north of east and rowing on the beam was awkward and painful. Our bodies were weakening and we still had a long way to go. After breakfast I switched on the satellite phone and read the messages as Ben rowed with one oar to prevent us sitting too square to the waves. The only message was from Tony, who had just arrived in

Mauritius to see in the four-man team who were less than a hundred miles from the island.

'He says it's a tropical paradise and we should hurry up.'

'He can be really annoying when he tries to banter with us; doesn't he know we only respond to praise?'

'I think he's trying to motivate us.'

'Weird.'

'It is a bit. He says he's organising their arrival party.'

'That's great. They're all going to be drinking beer in a couple of days, eating steak, having showers, not waking up all through the night to row.'

'Yeah, but we'll still be out here, having an adventure. I mean, would you rather be drinking cocktails and playing beach volleyball with a load of bikini-clad French chicks, and the girlfriends of course, or . . . be out here?'

'Arrgh, we need to get there!'

'Yeah, I suppose I should come and pull on those long plank things for a few hours, let me put on my foulies and I'll be out in a sec.'

'Alright. It's pretty much impossible to row, so pass me the logbook and I'll take our position down before we swap.'

I passed out the logbook and Ben clambered forward to where the GPS was mounted on the bulkhead and started jotting down our co-ordinates, which was part of our daily ritual. I lay back in the cabin pulling on my foul weather gear, swearing gently under my breath. When I was ready I opened the cabin door, put one leg out and immediately saw the large, cresting wave careering towards us. It seemed to come out of nowhere, far bigger and quicker than the others. For a second I was transfixed, a rabbit in headlights, as I said, 'Wow, shit.' It was going break on us. Immediately I was trying to get my leg back in and close the cabin door, but the wave was already upon us and with an almighty crash it hit us flush on the port stern.

We were sent sprawling onto the side and, although we didn't capsize, so much of the boat seemed to be underwater that we appeared to be sinking. Ben was standing in the footwell up to his waist in water. Where had the boat gone? It was listing so heavily to the side that it was half submerged. Everything on deck had washed off and was floating away.

'Quick, the water tanks!' I shouted, but I immediately had to slam the cabin door shut because we were so far over that the sea was flooding into the cabin. I sat down and had to watch Ben's blurred figure as he fearlessly lunged over the side to grab the two tanks we used to store our fresh water, which were drifting away on the frothing white aftermath of the wave. The foaming water was carrying off everything else from the deck that wasn't secured – our digital compass and the cushions we used to take the sting out of sitting on the hard wooden rowing seat. Having lugged the tanks back into the boat, Ben grabbed a bucket and started bailing out the water until the boat gradually started to reappear.

Trapped in the cabin, I assessed the damage inside. Everything was soaked. The footwell was full of water, the electrics were wet, the mattress sodden and everything that hadn't been in a dry bag was ruined. Luckily the satellite phone was safe, but the cabin lights weren't working nor were the iPods and shortwave radio.

When the boat was sitting up again I opened the cabin door and helped Ben bail out the water.

'Bloody hell, that was close. Are you okay?'

'Yeah, yeah, fine. Where the hell did that come from?'

'That was definitely a freak wave. The cabin is buggered;

everything is soaked, the mattress is waterlogged, which will make sleeping interesting.'

'I can't believe it. I thought that was it for a minute.'

'Yeah, my heart's still going like crazy. That was unbelievable.'

I started laughing, the nervous but relieved laughter of a close call.

Crouching down in the newly bailed footwell, Ben shook his head slowly in wonderment. 'That was really close,' he said, half to himself.

'Here, chuck us the camera and I'll get the aftermath of the Great Wave of day seventy-five,' I said, gesturing to the camera, which was secure in the side netting.

'What, right now?' he replied, dismissively. 'It's a bit much isn't it?'

He clearly thought I was mad to want to turn a camera on.

'My heart's still pumping; come on, that was pretty dramatic,' I said.

'Battery's gone,' he replied.

'Pass it here.'

He passed it and I switched it on, started describing what had happened and tried to get a comment out of Ben, but he gave me a withering look. Clearly I'd annoyed him. I suddenly had a flashback to being a journalist in Alderney. I hadn't been remotely over-zealous or pushy in getting people to speak, but if I thought something would make a good story I could get carried away, could get into trouble, like with the story about the guy in Guernsey who was caught having sex with a horse. I shouldn't have run that, not in a family paper and not accompanied with a fact box of other incidents of bestiality from around the world. Bad idea. Was I getting carried away again trying to film the aftermath of the wave before we'd even caught our breaths? Probably.

'Well, I guess I better get rowing. See you in a couple,' I said.

It was the fourth of July and we came to call this, our second worst disaster, the 'Independence Day Wave'.

48 From Bad to Worse

> 'One of those isolated waves which come from a
> great distance, strike with great force and, when they
> have moved on, leave behind an impression of
> comparative calm.'
>
> Bernard Moitessier, *Sailing to the Reefs*

After a couple of hours to calm down and reflect we agreed, during the next change-over, that we'd been pretty lucky to get away as lightly as we had and we managed to have a laugh about it.

'More or less dangerous than Ginga?' asked Ben, referring to the time we crashed a car into the Nile.

'Pretty close I think. That wave came out of nowhere and was so much bigger than the others.'

'Shame about the cabin light.'

'Yeah, that's going to make the nights interesting. Looks like we'll dressing by torchlight.'

'I know you like to look your best for the night shifts.'

'It's all about looking the part.'

'Right, I'll get rowing. I'm actually looking forward to the rowing now, with the cabin as wet as it is you can't get any sleep.'

I went into the cabin and lay down on the mattress. Soaking. Everything was wet and, with the overcast skies and choppy seas, it wouldn't be possible to dry anything out yet. I lay down, wetter than I had been while rowing. This was going to prove very uncomfortable. I closed my eyes and drifted in and out of sleep.

A couple of hours later I woke up to the sound of Ben swearing loudly. Then there was a sharp bang on the cabin door as a bungee cord was thrown at it, followed by more swearing. I put my head out of the door.

'What's going on?'

'The GPS is fucked, it's completely broken.'

The screen, whose comforting glow had formerly told us everything we needed to know about our position, speed and bearing, was a lifeless black. We tried everything, but having run through the electrics with the multi-meter it was clear that the unit had perished, no doubt as a result of being fully submerged earlier. Ben looked devastated. From the beginning he had loved the GPS and had been responsible for plugging in the waypoints we aimed for every hundred or so miles. I cast my mind back to Geraldton where he had said, 'As long as the GPS works we'll be okay.'

We found the small, handheld GPS we had brought along. Although it didn't give you as much information, it did give latitude and longitude, which we could plot on our charts. But there was more bad news. The stash of spare batteries we had in a supposedly waterproof bag was spoilt. We would have to rely on the batteries in the unit, which meant we could only turn it on once or twice a day. Although we would be able to find out where we were, we would have to row for twelve hours without knowing how fast we were going or exactly what effect the current was having on us. Also, we wouldn't have any warning of approaching ships.

In some ways it wasn't the end of the world. We would be rowing west as hard as we could and not knowing our position every minute of the day shouldn't make too much difference to our progress. But psychologically it was a real blow because we had spent 75 days looking at the GPS while we rowed, looking at our drift off course and making small adjustments to our bearing in response or gamefully setting down a target in one shift for the other person to beat in the next. As with so much technology, we had come to rely on it and now it was gone we were disorientated and unsure how effective the alternatives would be.

'Ah well,' I said, trying to be positive. 'The sun rises in the east and sets in the west, how hard can it be?'

But Ben was inconsolable and silently retreated to the cabin for his rest. As I rowed on I found I kept looking at the dead screen of the GPS every minute or so out of habit. It was annoying, but I wasn't that bothered. Why? I wondered. Was it out of relief that we were both unharmed or was it because I've always disliked computers anyway? Or was I reacting to Ben's gloom with a necessary amount of optimism? Had we become like some old married couple who manipulate their emotions to maintain a balance, just as seamen shift weight around a boat to find the perfect trim?

As night fell we fumbled with the two still-working torches to change over in the dark. After the drama of the day I was exhausted and kept falling asleep at the oars. Now that the adrenaline had worn off every muscle ached and, with the wet cabin making it impossible to sleep, we were both at a low ebb physically. Ben was sick in his last night shift and, at first light on Day 76, we realised it would be another overcast day and there'd be no drying out of the mattress or anything else from the cabin.

49 The Dark Boat

'The most terrific of all mortal disasters have imme-
morially and indiscriminately befallen tens and
hundreds of thousands of those who have gone upon
the waters; though but a moment's consideration
will teach, that however baby man may brag of his
science and skill, and however much, in a flattering
future, that science and skill may augment; yet for
ever and for ever, to the crack of doom, the sea will
insult and murder him, and pulverize the stateliest,
stiffest frigates he can make; nevertheless by the
continual repetition of these impressions, man has
lost that sense of the full awfulness of the sea which
aboriginally belongs to it.'

Herman Melville, *Moby Dick*

Day 76 was a dark day, both meteorologically and metaphoric-
ally. Ben fell in before lunch while balancing on the gunwales
to take a leak. Unsurprisingly, this didn't help his mood.
Fatigue and silence governed. At lunch, things went further
downhill. We switched on the satellite phone and there was
a message from Tony warning us not to go too far south. We
had told him what had happened, so were expecting him to
give us a bit of leeway as we got used to navigating without
the GPS on all the time. In addition, he'd been telling us for
the last two months not to get pushed too far north by the
prevailing trade winds. We thought the plan was to bank some
south when the wind was coming from north of east as it was

now. Tony was fantastically reliable and we liked him a lot, but his messages could frustrate us at times.

The next two messages didn't help either. One from Ben's mum and the next from his girlfriend saying they were worried about him and asking what was going on.

'Did you write about what happened yesterday in the blog?' he asked, obviously angered.

Oh dear. I had automatically detailed the Independence Day wave, with plenty of colourful detail, in the daily blog which I texted from the satellite phone. Now my instinct to record, document and report had once again got me into trouble.

'Of course, I mean it happened, didn't it?' That old journalistic chestnut: I'm only reporting a *fact*.

'That's not the point; you should have known it would worry them.'

I may have suspected that it would, but it was a good story that made a change from my usually humdrum daily updates. Still, maybe discretion would have been the better part of valour on this occasion.

As I rowed my afternoon shift the oars went through the water and the boat went forward, but all of a sudden she seemed a very different beast. When the GPS was working it had felt like a high-tech vessel, a purpose-built ocean rowing boat kitted out to a high specification with all the latest navigation kit, fully self-righting and with a watertight cabin. Now it seemed like a tiny rowing boat with no extras and a wet cabin. I still believed in her, that she could stand up to big weather and waves, even more so after the events of the day before, but suddenly she seemed plain and old fashioned.

People have crossed oceans on tiny rafts with no computer technology; didn't the Polynesians crisscross the Pacific in fairly basic boats? I thought. But then again, more must have died trying. How many had disappeared without a trace, trying to make land?

As I was thinking this, a large, grey dorsal fin appeared behind the boat. They say that sharks can smell fear and the appearance of this shark, refusing to show much of himself, seemed uncanny at best. The unwavering dorsal fin made straight for us then, a couple of feet off the stern, slunk under the surface of the sea. I peered over the side but saw nothing.

The atmosphere didn't improve in the night. Attempting to sleep on the waterlogged mattress was soul destroying, while rowing in the dark with only the compass still felt unnatural. On one night change-over I tried to make light of the situation but Ben was having none of it and was unconvinced when I said we'd be enjoying ourselves again in a few days' time.

Later that night we saw the light of a ship approaching. With no GPS to give us warning we'd have to keep our eyes peeled, especially with our backs turned to the way we were heading. It soon became clear that this ship would pass at a safe distance and we decided not to communicate with it. As she neared we could see they were sweeping the water with a searchlight. Clearly our AIS, a device which gave ships warning of our presence, was still giving off a signal and they were trying to work out what kind of a vessel was invisible at night. We flicked on the navigation light and called them up on the VHF radio. 'Are you okay?' they kindly wanted to know. 'Yes, we are fine,' we replied, but for the first time we weren't interested in prolonging the conversation.

50 Recovering Under a Bright Sun

'The sun, another lonely castaway, though the loftiest and the brightest.'

Herman Melville, *Moby Dick*

On the morning of Day 77 the sun shone brightly, burning off the cloud and bringing new hope, so after breakfast I got everything out of the cabin to dry it out. It took hours but when it was done the cabin was once again the most comfortable place in the world, and everything else started to look up too. Ben was in good spirits again and we resumed reading *Moby Dick*, which we'd stopped doing while we struggled to survive the last few days. When we turned on the satellite phone we discovered the forecast was poor, but it didn't matter because now we could lie down on a dry, sun-warmed mattress and sleep. News also came through that the four-man crew had finished. They hadn't got the record they'd so badly wanted but they'd finished all the same and were no doubt eating vast amounts of fresh, delicious food. We decided to try not to think about it and to put Mauritius out of our minds because we still had one thousand miles of open ocean to row and we would have to do it without the GPS.

However, there were some upsides to the whole GPS incident. It felt liberating not to have to look at the little blinking screen every few minutes. That evening we were treated to an incredible night sky full of stars, which was even more spectacular now that there was no light from the GPS to interfere.

The morning of Day 78 heralded the longest our boat had ever been at sea; it had done 77 days on the Atlantic with its previous owners. And, of course, it was the longest we'd been at sea for by about 77 days.

The next day we saw an extraordinary sight. As I rowed the first morning shift a city seemed to appear on the horizon. It was a sunny day and puffy white clouds skipped across the sky. I peered at the horizon, convinced I was hallucinating, as the tall spires of the floating town grew bigger and bigger. I woke Ben up and he came and watched on deck as the behemoth loomed into view. As it got closer we could see that it was a gigantic oil-drilling platform being towed across the ocean by a tug boat. We tried contacting them on the radio but got no reply. I filmed the surreal sight of the massive structure being tugged past us less than a mile away. It was visible for another half-hour before it shrank to a speck and disappeared.

Later that night we decided to have a longer sleep in the cabin to give our bodies a rest, as they were suffering badly from the salt sores. In the cabin we read *Moby Dick*, pausing to joke that perhaps we could get the record for the first rowing pair to drift across the Indian Ocean while reading.

51 'The Most Wondrous Phenomenon'

> 'We now gazed at the most wondrous phenomenon
> which the secret seas have hitherto revealed to
> mankind. A vast pulpy mass, furlongs in length and
> breadth, of a glancing cream-colour, lay floating on
> the water, innumerable long arms radiating from its
> centre, and curling and twisting like a nest of
> anacondas, as if blindly to clutch at any hapless
> object within reach.'
>
> Herman Melville, *Moby Dick*

Although we felt much better for our rest the next day, the oars moved heavily through the water and it felt like we were rowing through sludgy cement. When we turned on the hand-held GPS it confirmed that we had made little progress. There was nothing to do, though, but keep going.

The next day, Day 81, there was a thick grey cloud cover, which seemed to press down on us. With the clouds oppressively low, the air was dense and muggy. Day 82 saw the same relentless grey stretched above with not a hint of sky peeping through the blanket of gloomy cloud. A fine drizzle fell intermittently throughout the day but it didn't relieve the stifling atmosphere. With no light from moon or stars, these black nights made for disorientating rowing. Only the dim glow of the compass gave any sense of where we were heading and only the bright, irides-cent flashes of bioluminescence gave any visual suggestion of what was happening as the oars went through the water.

By daybreak on Day 83 we were praying for sun, but as the

murky dawn light started to glimmer we could see nothing but the endless bank of cloud. We continued to creep westwards until night fell and again not a hint of light lit up the sky. It was so dark it was impossible to see the difference between the sea and the sky, the horizon lost in a black oblivion. With everything inky and shapeless it was impossible to see our hands, which made rowing seem like an out-of-body experience. Only when we changed over and the torches were switched on could we see anything of the boat, ourselves or our surroundings.

'You're not going to believe this, there was a giant squid right by the boat,' Ben said, all excited, as I came out for my second night shift.

'Oh, wow. Is that a bit like the imaginary whales you saw on Day 6, the ones when I happened to be sleeping?'

'Don't give me that Mr "I-saw-a-full-lunar-eclipse". I'm completely serious, it was like a ghost in the water.'

'I did see a lunar eclipse, I'll prove it when we get back. We can look it up on the interweb.'

'Sure you can. Anyway, enjoy the rowing. It's basically impossible to see anything.'

'Apart from colossal squid, of course. I think you've been hallucinating.'

'See you in a couple.'

'Night.'

Having clambered into the rowing position, I started pulling away at the oars. It was so dark the minuscule flashes of bioluminescence were almost blinding. I had been rowing for barely five minutes when I saw it. Right next to the boat was the shimmering, pale, luminous bulk of a giant squid. I stayed deadly still, transfixed by this ghostly apparition. Its distended shape seemed to billow and contract as it gently rose and fell next to us.

'Ben,' I hissed in a loud whisper, 'it's back.'

I heard the cabin door creep open.

'I told you so,' said Ben.

It was hard to see clearly, but the whole undulating mass of the creature glowed dimly below the surface. It was about the size of a Jeep. Clearly it had come to the surface to feed on account of the absolute darkness. The dorado had certainly disappeared. We watched it for twenty minutes as it drifted in and out of view a few feet from the boat. Maybe it was watching us.

Later, after it was gone, I woke Ben up again because there were smaller schooling squid near the boat. These were around two or three feet in length but glowed in brilliant neon green and blue. Small groups of three or four appeared to hover in diagonal formation like ships of the line.

It felt like we were now passing through a sea of squid. A few days later a tiny squid jumped into the boat in broad daylight, no doubt in flight from a fish. Ben was rowing and the pale white creature fell at his feet.

'Ah, a jellyfish!' cried Ben.

'That's not a jellyfish, it's a squid. Amazing. Look at him! Well, shall we chuck him back in?' I said.

'I'm not touching that, it'll sting me.'

'Squid can't sting,' I said.

Ben bent down and tried to pick up the squid, but it immediately jetted out a cloud of ink.

We threw the squid back in and, as I took over the rowing, I wondered whether he was from a species of small squid or whether he was a few-weeks-old giant which would one day grow into one of the eerie monsters we had seen just days before.

52 On the Cultural and Natural History of the Squid

'Leviathan is not the biggest fish; I have heard of Krakens.'

Herman Melville, *Moby Dick*

Squid belong to the cephalopod family, members of which are among the earliest complex life forms known to have existed. The first cephalopods appeared 510 million years ago. Having survived various mass extinction events, they had time to evolve before the first dinosaurs appeared 225 million years ago. There are squid fossils from 150 million years ago, although their soft bodies mean that not many of these species of cephalopod survive in the fossil record, unlike the shelled cephalopods such as nautiloids and ammonites which are commonplace. Still, with their complex biology, squid have weathered many traumatic environmental events, including the one that destroyed the dinosaurs 65 million years ago.

Squid are ancient and adaptable. They're certainly older and more adaptable than us. The first human species appeared around six million years ago and modern Homo sapiens have only been around for 200,000 years. We are yet to be tested by a mass extinction event, but I suspect we'll struggle while the squid will swim on.

Scientists have successfully investigated smaller squid, octopus and cuttlefish, but the giant squid remain a relative mystery. Occasional sightings, strandings and even reported attacks involving giant squid have served to fuel the wide-spread legends of the Kraken that have been popular throughout most of recorded history.

With the explosion of whaling in the eighteenth century, people started to learn something of the giant squid – mainly because sperm whales dive to great depths in order to prey on them. When chased by the whalers, whales sometimes spat out half-eaten bits of squid. And when the crews caught the whales they could see circular marks and large scars all over the whales' bodies made by the sharp suckers on the tentacles of the squid. When the whales were cut open the men would find squid in their stomachs.

Then there were the sightings. Accounts describe how sperm whales were at times seen battling squid at the surface of the ocean. The whales would bite into the squid with their sharp teeth while the squid allegedly used their bodies to cover up the whales' blowholes and so suffocate them.

The rarity of these encounters between whalers and live squid filled them with meaning. In *Moby Dick*, Captain Ahab and his crew have just sailed into the Indian Ocean when they encounter a giant squid languishing at the surface. Mistaking it at distance for the white whale, they launch their rowing boats but on nearing discover what Melville describes as 'an unearthly, formless, chance-like apparition of life'.

The crew turn back to their ship, afraid and uncertain of the meaning of this latest development in their doomed voyage. As Melville goes on to say, 'Whatever the superstitions the Sperm whalemen in general have connected with the sight of this object, certain it is, that a glimpse of it being so very unusual, that circumstance has gone far to invest it with portentousness.'

Sperm whales also led modern-day scientists to the giant squid. By monitoring the depths they dive to and the areas they frequent, Japanese scientists were able to capture the first images of a live giant squid in the Pacific in 2005. Extraordinary pictures of the immense, alien-like creature attacking a baited line and losing a tentacle in the process confirmed that the giant squid is a solitary and ferocious hunter.

So much of the giant squid's world is still a mystery, but scientists can have learnt something of them from specimens such as 'Archie', a 28-foot creature caught off the Falkland Islands, which Tory and I went to see in the vaults of the Natural History Museum on a cold winter's day.

We learnt that the giant squid has been documented at up to forty-three feet in length. They have been found in the Atlantic, Indian and Pacific oceans. They have a mantle, or torso, containing their vital organs; eight arms with sharp suction cups; two longer hunting tentacles with large barbs; an exceptionally strong, parrot-like beak for eating; three hearts; a complex brain and nervous system and the largest eyes of any living creature, with the possible exception of the colossal squid.

Incidentally, the colossal squid lives in the waters of the Southern Ocean surrounding Antarctica and has been documented to grow up to forty-six feet in length. Remains recovered from these squid show that they eat sharks, toothed whales and other fish and squid species. At the other end of the spectrum, the pygmy squid grows to a length of one to two centimetres although it too is a ruthless hunter, enveloping shrimp in a ball of tentacles before munching through them with their beaks.

Cephalopods have an extraordinary biology, which makes them like no other creature. Their eyes have a camera lens like ours, but they have blue, copper-based blood as opposed to ours which is red and iron-based. They can survive in water with very low levels of oxygen, down at depths in which most fish would die. This is perhaps why the giant squid lurks in the deep during the day, a world where only sperm whales, who hold their breath for up to ninety minutes, can briefly visit to prey on them. No doubt their ability to live at these depths is what saw their ancestors through the trauma of the Permian–Triassic extinction event of 250 million years ago which wiped out 90 per cent of marine life.

The skills of cephalopods are many, varied and, I think, utterly weird. Under pressure they can jet out clouds of ink laced with dopamine, the chemical associated with sex and drug-addiction, which no doubt distracts predators. One species of squid blows out a cloud of phosphorescent colour to bamboozle its predators. Certain octopus can bite off or eat their own arms, should they become infected, and then regenerate new ones. With three-fifths of their brain located outside their central nervous system, in their skin and tentacles, cephalopods have otherworldly abilities. The footage captured by the Japanese scientists shows that the suckers on the tentacles will still sucker even when detached from the body of the squid and the whole tentacle will still move. Severed arms will continue to writhe and grab for hours, while all species show astonishing powers of colour change. These can be iridescent light shows or the more subtle ability to mimic, chameleon-like, their surroundings. They are capable of 'counter-shading', a skill in which the skin on the top half of the squid transmits the colour of the ocean below it, while the exact colour of the water above is transmitted by the bottom half of the squid, so as to make it invisible to predators from both below and above.

The most incredible feature of the cephalopods, though, is their intelligence. With their big, watchful eyes, squid, octopus and cuttlefish have intrigued scientists with their high levels of problem-solving and learning skills, with some even suggesting instances of 'tool use'.

The concept of intelligence in other animals is, of course, a difficult one but curiosity is normally agreed to be one of its central facets. Curiosity is the predator's friend, just as it is the survivor's. If you want to last for more than a 100 million years then you have to be either very lucky or willing to try new things.

Why had the giant squid appeared right next to us on that night of Day 83? Our guess was that they probably migrate to shallow water near the surface every night along with other deep-dwelling life forms. Perhaps the darkness of the starless and moonless night had caused the squid to overshoot. But right next to us? A 24-foot boat surrounded by the immensity of the ocean? It was disconcerting to think that we might be rowing over such an intelligent and totally alien predator. Night swimming was now definitely off. More than anything I felt a kind of humble euphoria. We had seen an extraordinarily rare and mysterious sight. As Melville has one of his characters say, 'The great live squid, which, they say, few whale-ships ever beheld, and returned to their ports to tell of.'

53 Para Anchor

'Mark, how when sailors in a dead calm bathe in
the open sea – mark how closely they hug their ship
and only coast along her sides.'

Herman Melville, *Moby Dick*

At 4.30 a.m. the wind turned against us and we were forced
to put the parachute anchor in to prevent ourselves being
blown backwards. With the navigation light and the torches
we managed to deploy it in the pitch black and then went to
sleep, annoyed at the hampering westerlies but relieved at the
chance for a rest.

When we emerged later that morning the cloud cover had
finally gone, burnt off by the sun. The same sea seemed so
different now; where it had been a dull grey under the cloud
it was now a vibrant blue with shafts of light illuminating the
deep azure.

'I'm going swimming,' I said.

'Okay, I'll keep a lookout.'

'A lookout for what?'

'Sharks.'

'Please, do you have to mention sharks when I'm about to
go swimming?'

'Sharks, killer whales, giant squid, they're everywhere.'

Ben was still off the swimming, believing, probably correctly,
that it made his salt sores worse. I couldn't resist, so I jumped
in wearing the mask and with the camera on a head strap. As

the bubbles dispersed I found myself staring face to face with a huge dorado. Incredible. It had the large forehead and bulldog features of a male and he swam right up to my face. For a second I panicked. He's going to bite my face off, I thought. Or worse, he'll dart down and bite something else off! But there he hovered, suspended right in front of my face, peering inquisitively at me. As I swam to the stern I saw five other dorado cruising around us at different depths. I could only see two pilot fish, though. Perhaps the others had been eaten or, bored by swimming so slowly, had mutinied to join some passing whale.

I worked away at the barnacles, which once again had spread to cover most of our hull. I carefully avoided the suckerfish that was still fastened to the boat, but there was no sign of the crab. Where has he gone? I asked myself and then, more worryingly, wondered if I was starting to consider crabs and fish as friends.

'Whale!' shouted Ben from the deck. I ducked under, scanning the blue with the camera but could see nothing as they were too far from the boat.

Later that afternoon I was in the cabin writing my journal when I heard Ben calling. He had just noticed that the retrieval line of the para anchor had come undone and was floating off. I had loosened the line because it was tugging and thus making the parachute collapse. Clearly I hadn't then done it up properly and now that the wind and sea had picked up the line had been pulled free and was floating off. I could see the orange retrieval line drifting away. It was now about forty metres from the boat.

'I'll swim for it,' I said, wanting to make up for not having done the knot properly but also confident that I'd get there and back – after all, I have my 100 metres badge.

'No way, it's too dangerous,' said Ben.

'It's fine; it's really not that far.'

'There's no way you're swimming that far from the boat. Anything could be out there; sharks, anything.'

'But if we don't get the retrieval line there'll be no way of getting the para anchor back in; we'll have to cut the rope and lose it.'

'We'll just pull it back in.'

'We won't be pulling it back in, it's already inflated; we'll be dragging ourselves to it.'

'Alright, we'll do that.'

'There's no way, we weigh over a ton,' I said and then, conclusively, 'I'm swimming,' with which I took off my cycling shorts and balanced on the side.

However, I could no longer see the retrieval line between the choppy waves.

'Don't swim, mate, it's too dangerous,' said Ben.

Ben put on a pair of sailing gloves and then proceeded with Herculean strength to drag our one-ton boat, hand over hand, fifty metres to where the para anchor was inflated. I put my shorts back on and, abashed, stood and coiled the rope, attaching it briefly to a cleat on the side of the boat every time the line starting fizzing back out. With his feet against the bulkhead, pushing his whole body into each tug, Ben said, in between puffs, 'Bloody hell, this is like landing a giant squid.'

54 Food, Glorious Food

'People think that if a man has undergone any hard-
ship, he should have a reward; but for my part, if I
have done the hardest possible day's work, and then
come to sit down in a corner and eat my supper
comfortably – why, then I don't think I deserve any
reward for my hard day's work – for am I not now
at peace? Is not my supper good? My peace and my
supper are my reward.'

Herman Melville, *Moby Dick*

Rowing for twelve hours a day makes you hungry. In the first
week we couldn't stomach the freeze-dried food, so most of
it went overboard. By the second week we'd identified a few
meals that we liked and we craved them. By halfway there
wasn't a meal that we wouldn't happily eat.

We spent all but the first few weeks totally obsessed with
food. Meals were the highlights of our day and the hungrier
we got as the trip wore on the more important food became.

I'd originally thought we'd be left with no chocolate for
later on in the journey, given Ben's frequent advocacy of
munching our way through the supplies. But I had no cause
to complain about this, since I allowed myself to be too easily
persuaded. There were differences between us, though. When
it came to chocolate, cigarettes, snacks and other luxuries, I
was all for squirreling away what we had and measuring it
out a little at a time so that it lasted the whole way. Ben was
more of the mind that if these things came in tiny measures

then they weren't fully enjoyable: it was better to eat the chocolate, smoke the fags, and be done with it. I would joke that he was dealing with issues from his Catholic upbringing and that after he finished everything he'd be wracked by guilt. He would counter that I was a mean-spirited Malvolio who thought that because I was sensible nobody else should have cakes and ale. But despite my Protestant upbringing, I did enjoy our little binges.

The difference in our personalities was well illustrated in the way we ate our breakfast every day. Ben would always opt for putting his chocolate bar in his porridge or muesli and feasting on everything at once. If I was making breakfast, I would say something like, 'And will sir be making his usual mistake?' To which he would always reply, 'Of course, and it's not a mistake.' I would keep my chocolate bar and eat it in instalments throughout the morning shift. Occasionally, as I put down my oars to nibble at the chocolate, I'd hear a voice roar from the cabin, 'Just get on with it!' by which my guilt-stricken and by now famished friend meant, of course, eating the chocolate, not rowing.

The basis of our diet was packets of freeze-dried food. These packs each contained about eight hundred calories and were dishes such as shepherd's pie or sweet and sour chicken. We simply hydrated them by adding boiling water. I say 'simply' but when the boat was pitching around in the waves the boiling water would often splash to scald a foot or the hydrating food would spill to soil the cabin. Then, having eaten half a meal, the unfortunate cook would have to sulk in a cabin that smelt of curry while tending to their burns. To supplement these freeze-dried meals we also had some wet meals, mainly based around the versatile baked bean, which tasted better but were lower in calories. Finally, we had various snacks and treats. Chocolate bars (gone by Day 85), peanut butter (we unceremoniously dipped our fingers in it for a couple of weeks until it ran out), sweets (amazing while they lasted), nuts (all six kilos went stale because we tried to separate them out), and pork scratchings (incredible texture after the freeze-dried sludge) were some of the choice items we had on board.

We also had drinks. The hot chocolate was gone by the end of the first month and we were left with tea. After a few weeks we ran out of sugar to put in the tea. This was probably for the best because we had stolen huge handfuls of sugar sachets from McDonald's, which meant that every time we made a cup of tea those alluring golden arches would trigger fantasies about eating a Big Mac, no three Big Macs, chips, nuggets, Coca-Cola and seven cheeseburgers. After the sugar ran out we used honey, then the syrup from the sticky toffee pudding and finally, when everything sweet was gone, whisky.

By Day 80 we had just about run out of everything apart from the packs of freeze-dried food. However, various meals were still tastier than others and these became our treats, the things we rewarded ourselves with, traded and dreamt about. We also had condiments: Tabasco, Marmite, olive oil, wasabi paste, mixed herbs and a seasoning sauce called Maggi. These went into pretty much everything. Of course, by Day 85 we'd run out of breakfasts, too, so we had to start eating puddings such as custard and mixed berries or rice pudding with cinnamon. When we ran out of these we started eating savoury dishes like bean and vegetable curry for breakfast, which we renamed the 'First Meal' to make it seem less weird. In fact, we took to renaming a lot of the meals so they had names which were closer to what they actually looked or tasted like. Chocolate chip pudding became chocolate mousse and potato and leek soup was mashed potato with chives or, most accurately, the 'horror'. By the end, though, we discovered that no dish was beyond redemption. Our bodies, knowing that we desperately needed the calories, were forcing us to like the foodstuffs it knew we needed. Invariably one of us would start to like a meal slightly earlier than the other, which would give rise to a conversation along the lines of:

'Hey, that's the third vegetable casserole I've seen you eat this week. I thought you hated them.'

'Oh, yeah, I do. I mean, they're pretty awful but they need using up.'

'I think I'll try one tomorrow.'

'I wouldn't, it'll only make you angry.'

The next day the suspicious party would eat a vegetable casserole and be instantaneously converted; the meal would shoot up through the ranks and become a 'classic'. It would then have a brief and stellar career before becoming totally extinct, a mere hunger-inducing memory.

55 Pain

'No man prefers to sleep two in a bed.'
Herman Melville, *Moby Dick*

We spent an uncomfortable night on the para anchor, with endless waves slapping the stern and disrupting our sleep. Top and tailing in the cabin was an awkward affair at the best of times, but heavy seas made it very difficult. Both of us would wake through the night to kick or hit the other person for snoring or putting their feet in the other's face. Ben would often accuse me of making loud blowing noises, like a whale spouting, although he actually did this himself a few times. This annoying habit was probably due to the stuffiness in the cabin, as we would have to tighten the air vents in rough weather to prevent water getting in.

Still, on Day 85 the wind had clocked around behind us so we pulled in the para anchor and got moving. When we switched on the handheld GPS after twelve hours of rowing we were elated to discover that we were going well at a consistent two knots. We carried on at this sort of speed for the next week or so, but this period became a drug-induced blur as pain finally took hold.

Ben had been taking painkillers on and off owing to the painful cramps he experienced as part of his ongoing nightmare with his bowels. Up until this point I had only taken them once. About a month in we had heard that the four-man team were all taking painkillers regularly and this had given Ben the permission he needed to start self-medicating. It was a Sunday and we were chatting before my four-hour shift.

'They're really effective, you should try one,' he advised.

'I'm aching a lot and the sores are stinging but I'm not sure it warrants painkillers.'

'They really do work.'

'Are you suggesting I take morphine-based painkillers recreationally?'

'Obviously your pain isn't as bad as mine.'

'Not at all, it's probably worse; I just have an incredibly high pain threshold.'

'Oh yeah, yeah. I remember when you pulled out of coming to the World Cheese Awards in the ExCel Centre because you had flu; you moaned about that for days.'

'Hey, flu is different and you know it.'

'Let me know when you start to feel some real pain.'

'Alright, give me one, fuck it, I'll take two, ten, whatever.'

I took one, looked at Ben, and said, 'That was a bad idea, wasn't it?'

For the next four hours I rowed, high as a kite, singing away. But what goes up must come down and later I vomited and felt deeply disappointed with myself.

By Day 85 we were in a very different situation altogether. I had experienced pain before, but I now had genuine problems. The salt sores, which appear in the crevices of the body, had worsened and the skin in my groin area was breaking and bleeding. It's worrying to see your balls in that sort of state. Our fresh water supply was limited because of using the manual watermaker and as a result we didn't make enough to wash the salt off as frequently as we would have liked. We even developed salt sores on our wrists where we dipped our hands in the sea to fill the jug to feed the watermaker. While my internal organs and muscles felt fitter and healthier than ever before, my skin was falling apart. The constant exposure to water kept it continually damp and therefore soft. Then the salt would grind away at the soft skin and disintegrate it. It felt like my skin was rusting. A few hours in the cabin before rowing again gave the body no time to recover. We had run out of surgical spirit to wash and cleanse, and so I had to turn to drugs for some respite.

Our conversations about medicine were as confused as our arguments about navigation. We both knew as little as each other. Ben had been to see a doctor in Ghana once who told him that the guidance on drug packets was always very conservative and that an average man should always take double. So I took four codeine, four paracetamol and a couple of tramadol. I can't remember a great deal about that week, but it wasn't fun. In the end Ben could see I was suffering badly and gave up his vitamin rations and rearranged the shifts to give me time for slightly longer, unbroken sleeps. It worked.

I often joked with Ben that he had to follow me around until he saved my life, like Morgan Freeman does with Kevin Costner in *Robin Hood: Prince of Thieves*, because of the one time I saved us from driving into an unlit parked lorry in Uganda. Here he really did save me; if not my life, then from a whole lot of pain that, if it had worsened, could have ruined the trip.

For the rest of our time at sea we made sure we used more of our fresh water rations to clean with and we also washed ourselves in passing rain showers, which would have been an interesting sight for any ships happening upon us. Despite, or perhaps because of, our individual trials with physical pain we were both determined, more than ever, to finish and we agreed that we would get to Mauritius even if one of us had to row the other one there.

56 One Hundred Days at Sea

'I am tormented with an everlasting itch for things remote.'

Herman Melville, *Moby Dick*

It wasn't just our bodies that were suffering – our brains seemed to be deteriorating too. We kept dropping or breaking things. We both managed to drop a bucket overboard, leaving us with just one, so we debated what we'd use to shit in if we lost that. None of the suggestions filled us with joy. We had dropped or broken all bar one of the spoon-fork hybrids we used to eat with. When we got down to our last spork we realised we would have to eat with spanners or use drill bits like chopsticks if the last one went. Which, on Day 91, it did when Ben broke it in half, but then rescued it by gluing the end of the spoon to the sheath of a knife, thus creating the first ever 'spife'.

On Day 98 we finished *Moby Dick*. Captain Ahab's fate is, of course, a lesson to all those who relentlessly follow their obsession. We still had a long way to go and I hoped we wouldn't suffer a similar fate. When we finished the book we lost something else – no more afternoon sessions reading aloud.

Two days later we celebrated one hundred days at sea. We were thin, hungry and heavily bearded but we'd survived for one hundred days in one of the toughest environments known to man. We had no mirror on board, so we took it in turns to describe what the other looked like. I started with a generous comparison.

'You look like a thin Oliver Reed in *Gladiator*, but your moustache is ridiculous, it's like General Melchett's from *Blackadder*.'

'I know, I keep getting food stuck in it; it's actually growing into my mouth now. As for you, you remind me of the Nazi officer at the end of *Indiana Jones and the Holy Grail* who ages really fast after he drinks from the Grail.'

'Thanks. So I basically look like a hundred-year-old iconoclastic war criminal. I think you'll find many other people liken me to Redford in his prime.'

Day 100 had crept up on us. When we started out, it seemed like an impossibly long time to spend in such a small boat. Given the 2009 pair's record of 102 days, we'd thought it was possible that we wouldn't even be at sea for 100 days, although we had brought enough food for 120. Now here we were: Day 100 and over five hundred miles to Mauritius. We still had a long way to go yet.

57 Longest at Sea

'For years he knows not the land; so that when he comes to it at last, it smells like another world, more strangely than the moon would to an Earthsman. With the landless gull, that at sunset folds her wings and is rocked to sleep between billows; so at nightfall, the Nantucketer, out of the sight of land, furls his sails, and lays him to his rest, while under his very pillow rush herds of walruses and whales.'

Herman Melville, *Moby Dick*

For me, one hundred days sounded longer than it felt. I felt more comfortable at sea after three months than I had after three weeks. It was as if I were rediscovering some dormant, primal symbiosis with the sea. Not many ocean rowers have spent one hundred days at sea. A pair on the popular mid-Atlantic route would expect to cross in around sixty days. However, solo rowers on the South Pacific can expect to spend close to a year in the big blue.

It's impossible to tell how a first-time ocean rower will react psychologically to being at sea; statistically, the highest drop-out rate comes in the first week. After this initial period people are less likely to give up, although they still do. As for second-time ocean rowers, there are very few. Only 32 of 519 people who have rowed oceans have done it again. These people have set the records for the longest periods at sea in an ocean rowing boat. The record for the longest single ocean row currently belongs to Erdun Eruc, who spent 312 days on the Pacific in 2007/08. As for the longest combined time spent at sea, the British rower Peter Bird clocked up an astounding 937 days at sea from seven rows, the bulk of which came from two long Pacific voyages. His seventh and final row (an attempt to cross the treacherous North Pacific) ended with his death at sea. The length of time he spent at sea, and his obsessive determination to be the first across many ocean routes, means that Bird in many ways resembles Captain Ahab, and he shares his fate. Clearly, ocean rowers and whalemen are connected by their desire to spend vast stretches of time in the wilds of the sea.

That's what struck me about the old whaling fleets of Melville's day: the sheer amount of time spent at sea. Although they would stop briefly to resupply at whaling stations, located on remote islands dotted around the globe, they were still gone from home for three or four years at a time. The oil they so brutally harvested from the sperm whale was preserved in barrels in the hold and they would keep sailing until the hold was full. Throughout the eighteenth and nineteenth centuries thousands of men were employed in this trade, each one of them spending years at sea. They were largely from Nantucket and elsewhere in New England, but European countries sent out whaling fleets too, most notably Britain and Holland. Of course, European maritime nations such as the British, French and Dutch also sent their men to sea for trade, war and exploration for years at a time, but few men went for as long as the whalers.

Moby Dick's narrator, Ishmael, who has set out on his first whaling voyage, recounts an extraordinary encounter that must have filled so many first-timers with awe and dread. He describes how, having left Nantucket and heading for the Cape of Good Hope, they chanced to cross paths with a returning whaler.

A wild sight it was to see her long-bearded look-outs at those three mastheads. They seemed clad in the skins of beasts, so torn and bepatched the raiment that had survived nearly four years' cruising. Standing in iron hoops nailed to the mast, they swayed and swung over a fathomless sea; and though, when the ship slowly glided close under our stern, we six men in the air came so nigh to each other that we might almost have leaped from the mast-heads of one ship to those of the other; yet those forlorn-looking fishermen, mildly eyeing us as they passed, said not one word to our look-outs.

Ishmael is amazed at the amount of time at sea the crews in his day endured, especially since these men were not press ganged as they might have been into the Royal Navy but had chosen to go, and for very little financial reward. He's astounded to see one man join up for another whaling voyage having only been back on land a matter of days.

I looked with sympathetic awe and fearfulness at the man, who in midwinter just landed from a four years' dangerous voyage, could so unrestingly push off again for still another tempestuous term. The land seemed scorching to his feet.

On reading this, we realised that there always have been and always will be people addicted to life at sea. Modern-day commercial shipping will rarely afford longer than a month or two at sea, as cargo ships can do a steady 14 knots in most weather. For them the world is a much smaller place than it is for the yachtsmen and women who spend months circumnavigating the world.

One man who found the lure of the open ocean irresistible was the French sailor Bernard Moitessier. He was leading the field in the final stretch of the first solo round the world yacht race in 1968. However, in his incomparable Gallic way, he made the decision to stop racing towards the finish line and instead head off two-thirds of the way around the world again to Tahiti. He recorded his decision thus: 'I have set a course for the Pacific again . . . I really felt sick at the thought of getting back to Europe again, back to the snake-pit . . . does it make sense to head for a place knowing you will have to leave your peace behind?'

The glory and considerable prize money went to the British sailor Robin Knox-Johnson, but Moitessier's decision won him another three months on the sea he loved so much.

The record for the longest uninterrupted period at sea is claimed by American yachtsman Reid Stowe, who in 2010 completed an epic 1,152 days at sea without touching land or being resupplied. Yachtsmen like Stowe, along with whalemen and ocean rowers, prepare meticulously for the extended periods they choose to spend at sea. So, perhaps even more impressive are those who find themselves adrift in small boats or fragile life-rafts without having planned or wanted it.

In 1820, a whaling ship named the *Essex* was rammed and sunk by an eighty-foot sperm whale in the Pacific. This incident was in part the inspiration for *Moby Dick*, but the tale of survival afterwards is perhaps even more extraordinary. The crew of the two surviving whaleboats, which are a similar size to an ocean rowing boat, were forced to resort to cannibalism in order to survive their 90-day and 95-day ordeals.

In the modern era there are many epic tales of survival. In 1972 a group of four adults and two children was cast adrift in a small open boat after their yacht was rammed and sunk by killer whales. Led by Dougal Robertson, they managed to survive 38 days until their rescue by using an array of clever but unpleasant techniques such as sucking the moisture out of fish eyes. In 1982 Steve Callahan survived for 76 days when his yacht sank a week out from the Canary Islands. Crossing the Atlantic with the prevailing winds and currents, he managed to stay alive in his life-raft by catching fish and seabirds. However, a Chinese sailor called Poon Lim is known to have survived for the longest time on a life-raft. He was working on a British merchant ship in the South Atlantic when it was torpedoed by a German U-boat during the Second World War. By collecting rain water and, among other ruses, catching and killing small sharks to drink their blood, Poon Lim managed an extraordinary 133 days at sea before being rescued by Brazilian fishermen.

These survivors tend to share a stubborn willpower along with a deep optimism – or at least hope – that they will be rescued. The human body is resilient, but the mind is so often fragile. Stay positive, don't give up, and take care of each other or, if you're alone, yourself; this is the mantra for anyone in a survival situation just as it is the key for anyone rowing an ocean.

The psychology of ocean rowing is, of course, slightly different in that rowers have made the choice to go and at least think themselves prepared for these long periods of time at sea. However, as they lose weight, kit starts to fail and land becomes a distant memory, many rowers find themselves in difficult survival situations. After all, what is an ocean rowing boat but a large, well-equipped life-raft?

Given the dangers of rowing and the cautionary stories of men such as Peter Bird meeting their death at sea, you may ask, is it worth it? Is it worth giving up your life in pursuit of something so ephemeral? For me the answer has to be yes, always yes. Even though, as some people pointed out, in the years before the row I had established a comfortable life in London with a good job. Did I really want to leave that all behind? Absolutely. Yes. I wouldn't be happy dying at the end of another three months of standing on the tube and sitting in front of a computer; but after one hundred days of beauty and danger on the wild sea? That would be worth it. I was free, and if you are going to enjoy the absolute freedom of life on the ocean, you have to accept in its entirety the possibility of death.

58 The Silent Sea

'The silence takes some getting used to but after a
while it's okay, you listen to your heart beating and
you listen to yourself breathing and when it rains
it sounds deafening.'

David Shrigley, *Let's Wrestle*

As anyone who has been in a coma knows, it tastes of salt
water. The efficient nurses of the intensive care unit clean
the respirator, which breathes for you, with a saline solution
that tastes like seawater. I remember lying there in 1995 as a
fourteen-year-old, unable to move, breathe, see or do
anything apart from smell, hear, taste and think. My body
stopped and only my brain went on, alone, trudging through
the black wilderness of paralysis.

Our perception of time is an inconstant thing, speeding up
gradually throughout our lives only to slow during the few
dramatic moments that punctuate our existence. For children
time goes slowly, the school year drags, the summer holidays
are a halcyon eternity, while the wait for Christmas lasts an
exhausting age. One study suggests that in terms of perception
of time a person living to the age of eighty will have lived
half their life by the time they reach fourteen.* As adults, we

---

* The 'proportional' theory first put forward in 1877 by Paul Janet states
that as you get older each year constitutes a smaller fraction of your life
as a whole and therefore is perceived to be shorter. So a child of ten feels

seem to lose months in a blur and then eventually the years themselves slip by.

Not if you're in a coma, though. When you can't move or see your senses are heightened. I remember smelling the autumn leaves on the nurses starting their shifts, feeling the cold glow in their cheeks receding. In the darkness of paralysis, time slows to a near halt until the brain starts to free itself and build palaces in the clouds.** Try it; close your eyes and lie motionless for ten minutes, it will feel like an hour. Try it for one hour, if you dare. You will not die of starvation or dehydration in an hour, so give it a go and feel the slowness of time and the infinity of your mind. Strange, you may think, and you would be right. I lay there for a month. After this, my time filled and sped up again with months of physiotherapy, tests, sickness, cures, doctors, nurses, patients being discharged or dying, wheelchairs, crutches, books, friends, foes, food and all the glorious chaos of life resuming.

Upon re-entering the 'real world' after my coma I noticed that the time human beings have freed up with modern

———————

a year as one-tenth of his whole life, while to a man of fifty the same is merely one-fiftieth of his whole life. If you start counting from the age of three, when most people's earliest memories start, then by the proportional theory if you live to eighty you have lived half your life by the age of fourteen. This is a purely mathematical theory and doesn't take into account other psychological factors, which we associate with time passing slower when we are young, such as the higher proportion of new experiences and higher level of learning. These factors are, of course, unquantifiable.

** Even Melville has something to say on this in *Moby Dick*: 'No man can ever feel his own identity aright except his eyes be closed; as if darkness were indeed the proper element of our essences, though light be more congenial to our clayey part.'

technology they have in turn filled with other devices that provide constant stimulation: television, computers, radio, mobile phones. People are rarely alone, rarely quiet. There is always the instant gratification of technology there to save you from spending any time alone and, God help you, by yourself. Of course, I got swept up in this and, apart from a few small rebellions, I watched *Neighbours* with the best of them. The terror and the pain of fighting for my life dissipated, as did the drama. They were replaced with the more mundane, and in many ways harder, struggle to overcome the physical after-effects of the illness. But also gone was the still and silence of that first month, which had been tempered by the rhythmic, mechanical breathing of the iron lung.

What I was left with, apart from a couple of lifeless feet, was a determination to experience, to live. I got at it, in the partying, travel, sport, books and friendships that followed in the years after. Experiences no different from anyone else's, but I cautioned myself to enjoy them and never forget where I *had* been. But I wasn't likely to forget. When I took up scuba diving the sound of the air being sucked from my tank reminded me of the hospital respirator, but now I was weight-less, drifting through the beauty and strangeness of the blue planet. If a shark were to bite my head off while I was diving I really wouldn't care because I was now swimming, free, through a wild ocean and not lying on a hospital bed in Tooting unable to wipe my own arse. And so it was with the rowing.

By Day 100 our GPS was broken, our food supplies were running low and the salt sores were agony. Time was slowing. I had no music to listen to, no GPS to look at every minute, no distractions. I was free and in the midst of the most wondrous place I'd ever been. The shock and fear at the start of the row had subsided into a meditative silence. But this time, instead of looking into the blackness of the backs of my eyelids or having them prised open to see a peering doctor behind the bright lights of the ward, now I could watch the immensity of the heavens and the vast blue ocean rolling away. Having known the silence of experiencing nothing, other than my own thoughts, for a month, the last 30 days at sea had been deafening. I felt unbelievably lucky. Was it worth dying for this experience? Absolutely.

I can't say if I appreciated spending so much time at sea in a small boat any more or any less than anyone else who has done it. I can't say if I appreciated it any more or less than the person I would have been if I hadn't been ill. All I can say is that it felt, at the time and afterwards, like a privilege.

59 The Beginning of the End

'For they say that, when cruising in an empty ship,
if you can get nothing better out of the world, get
a good dinner out of it, at the least.'

Herman Melville, *Moby Dick*

With over five hundred miles left we would need some help
from the weather if we were to get to Mauritius without
resorting to some very brutal rationing. Much of the food had
spoiled. We had enough for another two weeks, but to finish
our journey in this time would mean covering more distance
per day than we'd averaged up until this point, as Ben had
worked out while I was off in my own little dream world.

The good news was that strong south-easterlies were forecast; we'd just have to wait a few days for them. Before the
trade winds returned we had another calm to sit out, with
constantly changing currents too.

On Day 104 we came to a complete halt as we were treated
to what would be our last sight of an absolutely flat sea. Not
a ripple broke the surface of the water, which shimmered like
sheet-steel reflecting back the hazy white of the motionless
clouds. We stopped rowing for the day and organised the boat
for the south-easterlies, which would whip up this flat calm
into a furnace of tumultuous waves. It felt impossible to
connect the two seas to each other, their personalities and
faces were so different, but they were one and the same ocean.
We also spent the whole day making water so that we wouldn't

have to go to the trouble of doing this in the rough weather. As we did our tasks, I managed to finally film one of the dorados leaping out of the water. Then I filmed an even more extraordinary sight. At first I could barely believe my eyes.

Leaning over the side to film a dorado swimming in lazy loops underneath us, I noticed what looked like a pond skater skimming around on the surface. It was some sort of spider or insect.* I couldn't understand how its delicate frame survived even the smallest wave let alone a storm. How could something that looked as fragile as a daddy-long-legs survive out here?

Another new encounter was with a small shoal of unicorn leatherjackets. These dusty-coloured fish, with their upturned mouths and soft horns, appeared ghost-like out of the deep. They vanished and reappeared throughout the day, seemingly unable to make up their minds if they wanted to follow us or not. These fish, like the dorado, are helplessly attracted to floating objects. Juveniles often associate with jellyfish, while adults follow debris. The leatherjackets that sauntered silently up to us eventually decided not to associate with us. Perhaps we were too strange or maybe they had an existing bond with a nearby log. As it was the first time we'd seen them, I wondered if they might be a sign of land.

The next day while we were tucking into a breakfast of chilli con carne a ship appeared on the horizon. As it drew nearer

---

* Subsequent research has shown it was likely a sea-skater (*Halobates micans*), the only insect known to live out to sea away from coastal areas. They are essentially pelagic pond-skaters, spending their entire lives on the surface, feeding on fish eggs and larvae while they are preyed on by fish and birds. They lay their eggs on passing debris which, previously limited to occasional flotsam and jetsam, is now increasing as humans litter the oceans with plastic waste.

we were able to speak to the crew on the radio. Despite her course the ship came close enough that we could see the crew lining the deck to look at us. A rather panicked chief officer came over the crackly radio.

'Are you okay? What assistance do you require?'

'We're fine thanks; do you know the score of the Test match?' we asked, knowing that India and England were playing a series and having heard that England were winning.

'No, no, I only follow basketball,' teased the officer, who we'd assumed was Indian, though he must have known that England were winning.

'Are you sure you don't require any assistance?' he asked, sounding concerned again.

'We're fine, thank you. Where are you bound and what's your cargo?'

'We're bound for Japan with a cargo of Brazilian woodchips. And you?'

'We're bound for Mauritius with a cargo of facial hair and dreams.'

'Are you sure we can't help?'

'No, thank you, we've come a long way, from Australia, and if we accept any help it won't count as an official ocean row.'

'Okay, sir. We wish you good luck.'

'And to you; good luck and a safe passage.'

For lunch we both ate another chilli con carne. We were not only bored with the meals but also desperate for something sweet as our bodies had gone for weeks without sugar. For days Ben had been eyeing up the rubbish hatches where we were keeping the empty food packets. He was convinced there were some chocolate bars at the bottom. Over the last few days he had checked all but one, the smelliest.

'I'm going in,' he said.

'Don't do it to yourself, it's not good in there. Anyway, you've already said there's nothing in there.'

'I've got to check. I'm going in.'

He span the circular hatch cover open and immediately a pungent smell of rotting eggs poisoned the air.

'Ah, it's disgusting!' he cried, holding his nose with one hand as he started fishing out the festering months-old food packets. Then he screamed with joy. 'There's something in here! A Boost!'

Sitting at the bottom of the hatch was indeed a Boost bar. We had spent many long hours comparing the relative merits of Mars, Snickers and other chocolate bars, but nothing had come close to the Boost. As an all-round chocolate bar, the Boost is unassailable and we would often compose letters of praise to the food scientists who had developed it. We'd taken two hundred bars of chocolate in total, which was nowhere near enough. If we were to do it again we agreed that we would take enough for five per person per day. It had been a struggle to make our chocolate last until Day 85, and now it had been twenty days since we had eaten any. We washed the wrapper and went into the cabin. I cut, Ben chose. Then, over the next twenty minutes, we nibbled off the smallest segments and crumbs possible, letting each bit disintegrate on our tongues so as to get the most out of it. The chocolate was dense, milky, rich, complex – utterly mind-blowing.

'Do you know some Indians say you can spot a Westerner by the way they eat an orange?' said Ben.

'How so?'

'Because as we're chewing on one segment we're already peeling off the next one and putting it in our mouths.'

'Very true. So tell me, would you still make the mistake of melting your Boost into your porridge or would you enjoy it on its own?'

'Absolutely, the first breakfast I have in Mauritius I'll be asking the waiter to melt two Boosts into my porridge.'

'Yes, and refuse to eat it with anything but the "spife".'

Now that we were entering the final stretch all conversational roads led to Mauritius. What we'd eat and drink, whether we'd shower or bath first. In the end it was everything – we'd lie in the bath with the shower on, eating Boosts and drinking grog.

I was really looking forward to sleeping in a bed and eating a cooked breakfast, but what I was most looking forward to was seeing Tory. More than anything, her letters and messages and the very thought of her made the voyage so enjoyable. Mauritius on its own is just another tropical paradise, but the thing which made it so alluring for me was that Tory would be there. And I'd asked her to bring a fair few Boosts with her.

60 Second Storm

"'Avast Stubb,'" cried Starbuck, "let the Typhoon sing, and strike his harp here in our rigging; but if thou art a brave man thou will hold thy peace."

"But I am not a brave man; never said I was a brave man; I am a coward; and I sing to keep up my spirits. And I tell you what it is Mr Starbuck, there's no way to stop my singing in this world but to cut my throat.'"

Herman Melville, *Moby Dick*

When the weather finally came on Day 106 there was too much of it. The wind was too strong and the swell too hostile to make any serious progress. In the daytime the wind was around 30 to 35 knots and gusting stronger. At night it seemed to pick up further. Huge waves hit the boat and flung her off course, and the wind did the rest, pushing the boat onto the beam for us to be swamped by the next wave. The seas were as steep as we'd ever seen them. We were now wearing our lifejackets and clipping on all the time. Around teatime I was lying in the cabin when I felt the whole boat being picked up from the stern so steeply that I slid down to the cabin door. I heard Ben shouting and I opened the hatch. The deck was full of water slowly draining through the scuppers.

'Are you okay?'

'That was unbelievable, we nearly pitchpoled! Shit that was big.'

To pitchpole is to go head over heels. Only massive following seas can pitchpole a boat.

We were determined to make the best of this monumental weather, which we had been anticipating so keenly, and so we pushed on, silently enduring each increasingly scary shift at the oars. At dusk we switched on the handheld GPS. We discovered that we hadn't gone far and amazingly, despite pointing the boat in a north-westerly direction with southerly winds and swell behind us, we had still managed to slip south. The relentless currents seemed to be conspiring against us. We tried not to take it personally, but this weather seemed to possess a malevolent cruelty. As night fell we carried on, moon-light helping us to see the viscous, broiling seas around us. We both took to singing during these night shifts. The ocean was too loud to hear the other person singing, but the next day we told each other how we had sung to keep up our spirits amid the steep seas. I had plumped for hymns, 'For those in Peril on the Sea', 'Hark the Herald Angels Sing', that sort of thing, while Ben opted for popular musicals, madly chanting, 'A spoonful of sugar makes the medicine go down,' over and over again. With the sea bigger than we had ever experienced, we decided to put in a drogue for the first time. A drogue is like a small, more aqua-dynamic parachute anchor which, when deployed off the bow, keeps the boat in line with the following seas. It slows you down but lessens the risk of ending up on the beam and capsizing.

That night we both thought – not at all unreasonably – that we could have died. Luckily the boat hadn't rolled but it had come close, and recovering from a capsize in such violent seas would have been dangerous. We were therefore quite annoyed when we got a message from Tony asking why we were going south again and asking if we'd 'enjoyed our night in the cabin'. After putting the drogue in, we had retreated to the cabin and stayed there for the five or so hours until dawn. Was he bantering with us or was he being serious? Either way we were irritated; he was just looking at wind arrows on a screen, studying computer models, he had no idea what it was really like rowing on this beam sea and there was no way he could see what the currents were doing either. He had our best interests at heart, but we started deleting his messages instead of reading them to each other. We were losing our sense of perspective and our sense of humour.

Small things, which we might have found funny before, were now a source of major sense of humour failure. Going to the loo in big seas was always a precarious affair and whoever was sitting on the bucket was liable to be unceremoni-ously thrown off mid poo. On the morning of Day 107 I had to go. I watched the big seas nervously, waiting for the waves to abate. Is it getting calmer? I asked myself. Probably not, but a man's got to do what a man's got to do. I made a dash for it, positioned the bucket, pulled all my warm, dry waterproofs down and sat. A big wave hurtled along and slapped the cabin from the side, pushing the boat onto the beam. Oh dear, I'd better be quick. Too late, another wave was coming, a breaking wave, oh no . . . *smash*.

I screamed in rage. The wave had soaked me, drenching my foul weather gear, filling it with water.

The sea was rough all day and if it had a personality it wasn't a friendly one. The weather didn't let up over the next three days. We were continually wet and tired with the sheer effort of rowing in such violent seas. At night there was no moon or stars, only bouts of torrential rain. We decided to have the navigation light on. It didn't particularly help the person rowing to see anything, but the person in the cabin could see that the rower was there which, in such treacherous conditions, was some comfort. As I lay in the cabin at night

I watched the mad, demonic shapes cast by Ben's shadow as he got thrown about outside.

As we were getting nearer to our destination we started turning on the handheld GPS every two hours. We only had two hundred miles to go. The days seemed to be getting hotter, land felt close, but there were still no signs such as birds, other boats or planes.

But the handheld was now telling us that we were being pushed south, away from Mauritius.

61 Pilot Whales

'[The pilot whale's] voracity is well known, and from the circumstance that the inner angles of his lips are curved upwards, he carries an everlasting Mephistophelean grin on his face.'

Herman Melville, *Moby Dick*

On the morning of Day 111 the sun was shining in between the quick-moving white clouds. Drying and warming in the sun after another night of monsoon rains was like being born again. We'd eaten our breakfast of shepherd's pie in good humour and I was now rowing the first shift.

At first I could hear it only faintly. It sounded like a radio being tuned. I looked at the GPS wondering whether it had suddenly come to life. Ben opened the cabin door looking befuddled from his ten minutes of sleep.

'What's that noise? Is the GPS working?'

By now the noise had grown to a crescendo, so that by the time the whales arrived we were already looking out for them. A pod of pilot whales, about ten strong. Within no time they were all around us, the clicks, booms and whines of their sonar ringing in our ears. One breached next to the boat, its pitch black skin smooth and unblemished. Another big one, about fifteen feet long, came up for breath, its large blowhole letting out a deep, guttural exhalation. They were fast, moving around the boat like torpedoes. There was something ominous in their speed, their obvious strength and the way they surrounded us. There was nothing slow and ponderous about them; they moved like wolves or killer whales, fast and in a pack. I leant over the side and thrust the camera in, capturing one swimming right next to us. Then I spotted a small one, surely a baby, under the rudder, standing up on his tail, staring at us through the clear blue. I put the camera on deck and started stripping off but before I got my foulies off they had gone. These brief but beautiful encounters made all the pain worthwhile. They had arrived and disappeared so quickly, leaving us to our fate, but by now I didn't feel like we were imposters in their world; we were part of it, too.

62 Lunar Rainbow

'Somewhere over the rainbow,
Skies are blue,
And the dreams that you dare to dream,
Really do come true.'
     E. Y. Harburg, 'Over the Rainbow'

By Day 112 the only freeze-dried meals we had left were soup. So it was soup three times a day. At least there was still some choice, although chicken with vegetable won over potato and leek every time. We had also run out of toilet paper and I couldn't help but bring up the whole leaving-behind-the-big-pack-of-toilet-roll-in-Geraldton-for-no-apparent-reason thing with Ben. His ingenious solution was to cut up bandages from the medical kit into small sections. I tested them out at dawn as the sunrise was painting the wispy clouds in fiery hues of red, yellow and orange.

'I've got to hand it to you, they really work; they're soft, efficient, biodegradable. I think you could give Andrex a run for their money with these,' I conceded.

'See, I told you so.'

Although the weather had calmed down during the day it was still rough at night. Our biggest problem now seemed to be the rain. Dense clouds would unload relentless downpours on us and the wind and swell would always pick up for the duration. Some of these downpours were so heavy that whoever was rowing would have to stop and clamber to the bilge pump to empty out the water. It appeared that we were finishing our row in the African rainy season.

During the night of Day 113 we were rowing through these rain showers. One minute the bright, nearly full moon was casting a silvery light over the choppy waters; the next it had been blotted out by an immense rain cloud that unleashed a watery broadside for half an hour before passing on. In the middle of this process I saw an amazing sight, something I didn't know could happen. Having just weathered one drenching I pushed back my hood for some fresh air and there off our stern was a vast, milky arc glowing hazily in the moist night sky. Could it be that the moon's light was strong enough to illuminate a rainbow at night, could this be a 'moonbow'? Staring up at that eerie sight I was transfixed. I was sure I could see it, but I wondered if fatigue and hunger were inducing hallucinations. I later discovered that there is a phenomenon called the moonbow or lunar rainbow, which was first documented by Aristotle in 350 BC. But I didn't know this at the time, so the sight seemed like a mirage full of uncertain meaning. The next rain cloud to hit us was so heavy it thundered on the surface of the sea, calming the waves as the force of the falling rain beat down the swell. At these times we rowed valiantly on, but it felt like rowing through cement and it was virtually impossible to keep our eyes open. Lying in the cabin, listening to the drumming of the rain on the boat, was to lie in the comfort of knowing you weren't out there, at least not for a few more hours.

63 Nearing

'These warm Trade Winds, at least, that in the clear
heavens blow straight on . . . however the baser
currents of the sea may tack and turn.'

Herman Melville, *Moby Dick*

As the sun came up on the morning of Day 114 there were
signs of land all around and the sea seemed to be teeming
with life. Large clumps of seaweed floated through the
blue. There were flocks of small, white birds that were
either terns or tropicbirds. They hunted the silvery baitfish
that exploded out of the water, driven up by whales,
dolphins or sharks. It was hard to tell which; we only
caught occasional glimpses of fins and dark shadows
under the water. The dorado joined in the feeding, leaping
out of the water to give chase to fleeing fish. Our most
loyal companions were reminding us that they were still
around.

With fewer than one hundred miles to go to Mauritius,
the current had come behind us at last and we were
making good progress north. We needed to get to the
northern tip of the island and, with easterlies forecast, I
said we should head up and get on the same latitude as
the finishing line. After some debate Ben agreed and we
rowed with a more northerly course. But we were soon
admonished by Tony who was afraid we would overshoot
the northern tip of the island. He said our course left us

with 'diminishing angles' and that it made no sense to go north then west, we should instead head a steady north-west. In a yacht perhaps, but we'd been rowing for long enough now to know that it's easier to maintain a latitude than to try and reach one against a current. Still, we bowed to his greater experience; after all, approaching land in an ocean rowing boat with limited ability to manoeuvre is dangerous and we'd never done it before. Had we trusted our instincts, though, we might not have got into the trouble we did when, inevitably, the current turned against us.

This happened during the night of Day 114. The easterly wind picked up, the current started pushing us south and we were back in the washing machine, only instead of having three thousand miles to play with we now only had about fifty; now every mile mattered. Physically it was the hardest night rowing we did. I rowed the entire night with one oar. That's two hands pulling on one oar for six hours just to try and keep the boat on course for Mauritius.

When daylight arrived on Day 115 we were both knackered. We had run out of fresh water and, unsurprisingly, the watermaker had packed in again. We got out the handheld pump and started pumping enough water to hydrate our breakfast soup. Only potato and leek left now, but we didn't care; we knew how close we were and were hoping that if we rowed together maybe we could punch through the current and get to the safe port at the north of the island. That's where our loved ones were, waiting with Boosts and beers.

I knew that Tory had arrived the night before; she was now only forty-odd miles away. It's not hard to imagine how this thought motivated me through the hardships of those last few days. Since she was on the same time zone I decided to call her after breakfast to check she'd got in safely. She picked up straight away.

'Hi, darling, are you okay?'

'Yeah, we're fine, not far to go now. Did you remember the Boosts?'

'Of course, but are you alright out there? The wind is really strong here, the palm trees are getting blown flat; it must be a nightmare out there.'

'It's not too bad. Really, it's fine.'

Ben raised his eyebrows at me and I shrugged as if to say, 'What else can I say?' As I said goodbye I felt the excitement of being reunited with Tory. I had imagined it so many times and now it was just around the corner. We really were on the home straight, with only another day or two to go.

We tried rowing together through the daylight hours of Day 115. Rowing without breaks was tiring, but we were making little headway north and had worked our way halfway up the coast of the island, although it remained out of sight.

During the afternoon a car carrier passed by less than half a mile away. We could see the foaming white of the bow wave it made. We were definitely close to land now and we could see for the first time in months the white trails of planes slanting across the blue sky.

At night we decided to revert to our usual shift patterns so that we could rest before the final push north. That night was another tough one, with the currents preventing us moving north. For every mile we went north we would go three west. We were fast running out of space in which to manoeuvre the boat towards the island's northerly port.

At dawn on Day 116 we had sixteen miles left to get to the

north of the island but only about twenty left before the strong easterlies pushed us onto the treacherous coral reefs that line the eastern coast of Mauritius.

PART THREE

The Last Day

64 False Start

'Warmest climes but nurse the cruellest fangs.'
Herman Melville, *Moby Dick*

On the morning of Day 116 we readied ourselves for what would be our joint big effort. We would have to row together all day to get to the safe port on the northern tip of the island. We only had enough water to hydrate one meal, so we shared our last potato and leek soup. It didn't matter, we agreed; that night we'd be eating steak, chocolate and whatever else we wanted. Still, it was hard to ignore the pangs of hunger as we set off together, rowing as hard as we could.

The wind and swell was all coming from an easterly direction, so we once again found ourselves rowing on a beam sea as we headed north. A fitting way to end, we joked. After the first hour we turned on the GPS but, despite rowing together, it told the same story. We had only edged north while flying three miles west. The current pushing us south was brutal, but the wind and waves were unrelenting in pushing us west towards the reefs off the east coast of Mauritius. We looked at the chart and spoke to Tony; we knew we could do nothing but carry on.

On we rowed, all the time looking to our right to see if we could see the island. We knew that, as a mountainous, volcanic island, Mauritius would probably be covered in cloud and we might not see her until we were relatively close, perhaps as close as twelve miles, we'd heard. Ben was convinced he could smell the island.

'I can definitely smell it. I can actually smell land.'

I sniffed at the air but couldn't smell anything.

'There! There it is, land ahoy!' cried Ben, pointing at the horizon.

I stopped rowing and stared. I couldn't see anything.

'There,' said Ben, pointing to what I thought were some dark clouds.

'What, those clouds over there? Oh . . . yes, I see it! Shit, that's seriously close!'

'It looks like Jurassic Park!'

There it was; the hazy outline of the steep pinnacles of rock. It was a strange and incongruous sight after so many days at sea. The island also seemed huge and dangerous. A safe harbour was there, but we still needed to find it among the rocks and reefs.

Exhilarated, we rowed on, looking over our shoulders every few minutes to make sure we hadn't imagined our sight of land. After another hour we turned on the GPS but it told the same story. We had gone less than half a mile north and three miles west.

We couldn't go on like this. We only had twelve miles left now before we hit the east coast. It was 10 a.m. so at the current rate we would hit the coast by 2 p.m. We realised that we couldn't stay out another night with the conditions moving us as they were, but we really didn't want to accept a tow. After nearly four months at sea, rowing every day, we had to row ourselves in. We looked at the chart: there were small gaps in the reef; surely we could aim for one of those.

I called Tony on the satellite phone while Ben carried on rowing.

'What's happening? You're still losing way too much west,' he said, sounding concerned.

'We're rowing two up and pointing her due north. It's the same as yesterday – the current is too strong.'

'Can't you point her north-east?'

'What, back out to sea?'

'If that's what it takes.'

'We've got fifteen knots of wind from the east; we can't row north-east. Can't we look at coming in somewhere else?'

'Alright. Let me speak to some of the guys here at the yacht club, they know the waters. I'll call you back in ten.'

As I was recounting the conversation to Ben a shearwater fluttered down before coming to rest on his oar. It paused, looked at us and then took off. As we looked out after it we spotted two albatross. With their huge wingspan, the biggest of any bird, these black and white creatures looked huge and foreboding. I grabbed the camera and filmed them hovering, motionless and watchful. Then they disappeared, gliding away on the blustery winds. Another of the strange, beautiful sights of the life at sea we were soon to leave behind. Surely this was a sign we said, only half in jest.

In Coleridge's poem *The Rime of the Ancient Mariner*, the crew of a ship are doomed after one of them shoots an albatross. Incidentally, the poem wasn't an instant classic, and Coleridge's publisher told him most of the initial sales were from seamen who mistakenly thought they were buying a book of traditional nautical songs.

Tony called back and confirmed that there was a gap in the reef at the southern point of the island. It was a narrow one but led to an old harbour, the Grand Port. We would have further to go, but by turning south-west we would have wind and current behind us so if we rowed hard we should make it just before nightfall. Tony gave us the co-ordinates and said that he would watch our progress before coming out to meet us on a boat with friends and family. Then we could follow the speedboat through the precarious, winding opening in the coral. We arranged to speak again on the phone when we could see the lighthouse that marked the entrance through the reef. Finally he warned us not to stray too far out to sea lest the north to south current overshoot us beyond the entrance, but at the same time to come no closer than two hundred metres to the lighthouse.

We were elated. We would be able to row in after all, with our bodies and our pride intact.

Turning the boat around, we immediately noticed the difference. Now we were surfing again, cresting gently down the waves. We turned the GPS on after an hour and discovered that we were doing just over three knots. At that rate we should get there by dusk. We picked up the pace, rowing with all our strength for the Grand Port.

65 The Battle of Grand Port

'Firstly you must always implicitly obey orders, without attempting to form any opinion of your own regarding their propriety. Secondly, you must consider every man your enemy who speaks ill of your king; and thirdly you must hate a Frenchman as you hate the devil.'

Lord Nelson, 1793

Two hundred and one years, almost to the day, before we arrived at the Grand Port there was a devastating naval battle there between two old foes.

Discovered by the Portuguese, the uninhabited, volcanic island of Mauritius was first settled by the Dutch. They occupied the island in 1638 and, by the time they left in 1710, the tame, flightless dodo was extinct. The Dutch left the island to a ragtag band of slaves, renegades and pirates until the French decided to claim it in 1722. The island prospered as a refuelling station and the French grew sugar, cotton and indigo there. However, they also used it as a base from which to harass British shipping moving to and from their imperial positions in India. The problem was such that William Pitt declared: 'As long as the French hold Ile de France [Mauritius], the British will never be master of India.'

War against Napoleon in Europe galvanised the British into action. After the victory of Trafalgar in 1805 and the consequent British naval supremacy, it was an embarrassment that the French could still cause so much havoc in the Indian Ocean. In 1810, the British decided to invade.

The first phase of the action was Commodore Josias Rowley's successful invasion of the neighbouring island of Réunion, which had been under French control. Rowley then dispatched four ships to Mauritius. *Iphigenia* and *Magicienne* were to blockade Port Louis, while the 38-gun *Sirius* and the 36-gun *Nereide* were to establish a foothold at the Grand Port. *Sirius* was under the control of the bungling Captain Samuel Pym, while the *Nereide* was commanded by the extraordinary Captain Nesbit Willoughby. At the age of 31 he had twice survived court martial for insubordination and had developed a reputation as an aristocrat who shot first and asked questions later. After a number of close scrapes, including an explosion that disfigured him, his men started calling him 'the Immortal' for his apparent invincibility.

On 13 August 1810 they took Ile de la Passe, a tiny island on the lip of the reef guarding the southern entrance into the Grand Port. Pym, in *Sirius,* then went off to join the blockade while Willoughby began distributing propaganda to the local populace to warn of the imminent invasion.

Then on 20 August, while halfway up the east coast, Willoughby sighted two French warships returning with three captured East Indiaman vessels. He had a hard five-hour row to get back to Ile de la Passe where he manned the small battery and, flying French colours, lured the ships in. When in range he hoisted the Union Jack and opened fire. Things were going his way until an explosion took five of his cannons out of action and gave the French captains the chance to sail their ships into the safety of the Grand Port along with two of their East Indiaman prizes, while the third escaped.

With the French ships bottled up in the old port Willoughby sent word to Pym, who sailed back with the other British ships to attack. He arrived two days later and, on board the *Nereide*, the two captains once again argued about who would go first into battle. Pym took precedence as the senior officer and started out through the treacherous channel but quickly became stuck on the coral reef. It took all night to free the ship and the next day they decided on a change in tactics. This time Willoughby would lead with the help of a local black Mauritian, who would use his knowledge of the waters to pilot the *Nereide* through. The other three frigates would follow in Willoughby's wake.

As the *Nereide* was negotiating the shallows, Pym, unable to stomach the indignity of following Willoughby into battle, steered out of his wake as if to overtake. Almost immediately his ship ran aground and was soon taking on water. Behind her the *Magicienne* also became lodged on the reef. The *Iphigenia* got through and let off one broadside before losing her anchor cable, drifting behind *Nereide* and out of the action. This left Willoughby on the *Nereide*, now woefully outgunned. Willoughby then did what any self-respecting Royal Navy officer of his time, who had been in service from the age of twelve, would have done. He parked his ship 200 yards from the largest French ship (the 44-gun *Bellone*), nailed his colours to the mast and opened fire.

Under her previous captain, the *Nereide* had gained a reputation as the harshest ship afloat, with men given the lash for any number of petty offences. Now her crew met with a new hell as the ship was raked again and again with cannon fire. A flying splinter gouged out Willoughby's left eye and he was taken below while the barrage continued. They inflicted significant damage and casualties on the French ships, but there were soon too few able-bodied men to return fire and the *Nereide*'s guns fell silent.

The next morning the dawn light illuminated the scene of

carnage as hundreds of bodies floated amid the debris of the crippled ships. Willoughby would later take a grisly pride in the extraordinary death toll. Of the 281 men on board there were 230 casualties. Four out of every five men had died; a terrible toll compared to the one in every six on Nelson's *Victory* at the battle of Trafalgar.

When the French boarded the *Nereide* they found Willoughby, barely conscious, wrapped in the Union Flag. But this wasn't the end of 'the Immortal'. He was taken to a French hospital and laid next to the French Captain, Duperré, who was recovering from a grapeshot wound. The two got on famously, shaking hands and deconstructing the battle they had just waged against one another. When the French governor ordered that Willoughby be shot for the crime of sedition (his earlier distribution of propaganda) Duperré interceded so that once again 'the Immortal' survived.*

In November, Rowley commanded a successful invasion of the island, landing troops at the bay in the north and encountering very little resistance. This eventual success

---

* Back in London the doctors deemed him unfit for naval service. With more than a little of the Ahab about him Willoughby decided he would not be held back by his broken body and so went to Russia where in 1812 he talked his way into commanding one of their cavalry regiments against Napoleon. He was then captured by the French and imprisoned for nine months but predictably managed to escape. Seeing the error of their ways the Navy re-instated him and he rose to the rank of Rear-Admiral of the White. He died in 1849 and the Annual Register recorded that: 'He was eleven times wounded with balls, three times with splinters, and cut in every part of his body with sabres and tomahawks: his face was disfigured by explosions of gunpowder, and he lost an eye and had part of his neck and jaw shot away . . . and at Leipzig had his right arm shattered by cannon shot.'

saved face and allowed the British officers to write off the disastrous engagement at Grand Port as a minor yet wholly noble encounter. 'A glorious resistance almost unparalleled even in the brilliant annals of the British Navy,' was how the contemporary commander of the Cape fleet described it. This habit of turning bloody defeats into victories of the British spirit would continue down the years. For men such as Willoughby it would always be better to go down fighting and, as subsequent history shows, there would always be men like Willoughby prepared to fight.

Now *we* were rowing towards the Grand Port, where the coral lurks beneath the surface of the sea like so many jagged gravestones for the hundreds of sailors whose bones lie at the bottom. The weather had denied us a safe entry to the northern port. Instead, we were rowing towards the Grand Port, the scene of one the bloodiest defeats in British naval history. Had pride not been at stake, Willoughby could have surrendered and if pride had not been at stake perhaps we could have requested an early rescue when it became clear that we wouldn't get into the northern bay. But we wanted the glory of rowing from land to land. So on we rowed, towards the southern entrance of the Grand Port, unaware at the time that this was the scene of so much carnage exactly two hundred and one years before.

66 The Final Furlong

'It is only when caught in the swift sudden turn of death, that mortals realise the silent, subtle, ever-present perils of life. And if you be a philosopher, though seated in a whale-boat, you would not at heart feel one whit more of terror, than though seated before your evening fire with a poker, and not a harpoon, by your side.'

Herman Melville, *Moby Dick*

As we raced towards Grand Port I was amazed at just how hard we could row. After four months at sea we had lost a lot of weight, nearly three stone between us, but we still pulled on the oars like a pair possessed. In part it was the adrenaline of closing in on land, the emotion and exhilaration of nearing our loved ones that spurred us on. But I also knew it would be the last time I rowed and therefore I put everything into it physically, as if to prove to myself that I could. I didn't worry about overdoing it because that night I knew I would be in a soft, dry and luxurious bed. No doubt there would be a mini bar and room service, so going without lunch and dinner wouldn't matter either. Soon we would be there.

Despite the excitement of our imminent finish, I was also sad. Leaving behind our life on the sea would be hard. The 'real world' would have to be re-engaged, money would have to be chased, public transport caught, bills paid and all manner of difficult decisions made. I knew I would miss the rhythm and elemental beauty of life at sea, the only life I had known for months.

As we neared the southern tip of Mauritius, the island came into focus, its verdant green slopes now clearly visible. I could smell the land; its lush, dense aroma filled the air enticingly.

One of Ben's rowlocks had come loose. The only serviceable spanner had been rounded off by our late-night fixes over the last few stormy weeks. Still, it only had to hold up for another few hours so we rowed on, ignoring the clatter and din of grinding steel.

We discussed more important matters instead, like who was going to tidy the cabin before we got to land. Both mothers would be there and wouldn't be impressed with what they saw. As the lighthouse came into clear focus we realised we were nearly there. We took it in turns to go into the cabin to prepare for arrival. Nothing could be done about the beards, but we cleaned our teeth, combed our matted hair as best we could and looked out our passports. I picked up a toy kangaroo I'd got for Tory in Australia and put it into the pocket of my foulies. Finally I tied a small Union Jack to one of the antennae. We had the camera on deck to film our arrival and we also had the flares in a waterproof bag. In Australia, Tony had warned us not to let off the flares on entering the northern bay in Mauritius in case one fell on and set fire to someone's yacht. But we had been planning to disregard that particular bit of advice and set off a fireworks display big enough to let the whole island know we'd arrived.

The disused lighthouse was very clear now. It stood like a bony white finger of warning about five hundred metres away. In line with the lighthouse were the reefs outlined by the white water that broke over them in jagged lines. About a mile behind the reefs were the tall, green mountains of Mauritius.

The weather seemed to be deteriorating. The sky was grey and the air seemed to hum and crackle with invisible electricity. We could see the breaking waves on the reefs around and behind the lighthouse, which jutted out on a rocky spit.

'We're getting too close,' warned Ben.

'This is right; we don't want to overshoot the entrance. I've checked the chart and it's very narrow,' I replied.

'But look at those breaking waves, they're pretty big.'

'Tony said two hundred metres, we've got to go closer,' I argued back.

Suddenly it was becoming quite tense. The atmosphere around us was alive with dense energy. Now we could hear the thunder of the waves on the reefs and feel the current dragging us mercilessly south. It was about 5 p.m. and the light was starting to fade behind the grey clouds. The GPS was on permanently, but we were still outside the co-ordinates.

Then the phone went. It was Tony. He sounded nervous.

'How is it out there?'

'It's okay, we're getting close now,' I replied.

'Okay, you need to stay at least *three* hundred metres away from the lighthouse now the weather is picking up.'

'Okay.'

'We're coming in a boat so we should be at the gap in ten minutes. We'll come out into the open sea and find you, okay.'

'Brilliant, we'll see you then.'

'Listen, if it's too rough out there we are going to have to tow you. If these cyclonic conditions build it won't be safe to row through the gap, it's too small. Okay?'

'Understood. We'll see you soon.'

I recounted this to Ben and we carried on rowing, but now only edging our way south, nervously checking the GPS every minute. We were on a beam sea heading south, but there were no waves big enough to come over the side, not even a splash. The only thing that made us nervous was looking landward and seeing the white water on the rocks. Ten minutes went by and the atmosphere was now charged with pressure. We'd lost a little ground towards the coast but not much.

'Where are they?' said Ben, agitated.

'Okay, you keep rowing and I'll keep a look out,' I said, standing up.

I stood with my back to the cabin, peering out to where they should be. There were still no breaking waves but it was choppy and we rose and fell in and out of the swell, which charged towards land.

Then it appeared. Out of nowhere a breaking wave bigger than anything we'd seen in the last 116 days was churning towards us with a guttural rumble. I knew immediately it would roll us. The white water alone was higher than us; it was going to engulf us in seconds.

'Oh no . . .' I said quietly. I turned to Ben and he was looking back at me with an expression that mixed disbelief with a kind of pained inconvenience. It was an expression that said, 'Really, after all of this?'

I quickly turned and closed the doors of the hatch tight and held on to the steel roll bars. Glancing over my shoulder, I saw Ben take his feet out of the straps of the footplate and reach his hands out for the gunwales to brace himself for the impact.

Now we're going to die, I thought as the wall of white water arrived. My veins coursed with adrenaline.

For a moment the sea in front of the wave looked still and pure, so peaceful and blue in contrast with the white rolling mass that was now seconds away. But already the flat in front of the wave was being disturbed and soiled by spitting shards of tumbling white water. The noise grew suddenly louder, from a rumbling hiss to a raging thunder as the turmoil of water reached us.

Now we really are, actually, definitely, after all of this, after everything, going to die, I thought. *Typical.* As for words, the only one I could manage in time, the only one that seemed appropriate, was: 'Shit!'

I took a deep breath.

The wave hit us with a violent, sickening crash and everything went black.

67 Decisions

'Now, in general, Stick to the boat, is your true motto
in whaling; but cases will sometimes happen when
Leap from the boat, is still better.'
                                    Herman Melville, *Moby Dick*

I came up in the bubbling, foamy aftermath of the wave. The
boat had self-righted and languished about fifteen feet away
from me. I could see Ben. He was only about six feet from
the boat.

'Swim to the boat!' he shouted.

I swam desperately to the boat. The flat water was still alive
with the energy of the disappearing wave, fizzing and hissing
as it calmed. Debris from the boat floated everywhere.

I felt relief to be alive and, despite the violence of the capsize,
not even injured. I was also relieved that we hadn't been
clipped on, otherwise the lines would have tangled around
the boat and we would have run a greater risk of being smashed
against it. But fear immediately pushed relief out of the way.
This is really bad, I thought. I started swimming heavy strokes
in my foulies. I couldn't help but feel some pride that the boat
had self-righted. We had been right to increase the ballast.
'Don't think about that, you idiot!' a voice screamed in my
mind. The foulies were too heavy in the water so I quickly
pulled down the zip and slipped out of them. Now wearing
nothing but cycling shorts, I made the boat within a few
seconds.

Flopping over the side into the hole where the bow seat should have been, I was greeted with a scene of utter destruction. All the oars had been broken or carried away, the lifejackets were gone, the seats ripped out, antennae snapped, rowlocks bent and everything from the deck had been washed away.

Ben's long matted hair was falling wildly over his face and his waterlogged beard was dripping.

'The flares!' I shouted.

I jumped back into the sea and swam to the flares, which were floating off in a watertight bag. I managed to get to them and back to the boat in what felt like seconds. I clambered back in. We had lost a lot of ground towards the lighthouse and it now loomed over us perilously.

'Where the fuck is Tony?' shouted Ben.

'They should be close. Let's set off the parachute flares,' I said, catching my breath.

'Yeah, I looked in the cabin and it's upside down. The batteries have come out the sat phone and it's all smashed up.'

'Okay, here we go,' I said, passing Ben a parachute flare and taking one for myself.

Readying the flare I pointed it upwards and pulled the cord. The fizzing, iridescent ball of fire shot vertically into the air with an angry hiss. At the same time the canister kicked back in my hands and the metal cap backfired, cutting my finger on the knuckle.

'Ouch! My finger!' I said, cradling my finger as blood trickled down my hand.

'Are you okay?'

'Yeah, fine, but be careful. They backfire.'

Ben held his flare away from his body and pulled the cord. It shot into the sky leaving a brilliant wake of glowing red. At the same moment I doubled over in pain. The metal cap had shot back and hit me flush on the shinbone.

'Shit, mate, for fuck's sake! Owww! You shot me with the discharge!'

'Oh, sorry. Are you okay?'

I looked at my shin and saw the perfect double hole it had cut in my leg. In the deeper hole I could see the bone, white against the moist red circle of flesh that surrounded it. Then the blood started streaming down my leg. Looking at the blood I suddenly felt very tired. I covered the wound with my hands but could feel the thudding of blood pumping through the hole.

'Ouch, my leg, that really fucking hurts,' I said, wincing.

'Where the fuck is Tony?'

'Mate, do another flare!'

Ben grabbed one of the parachute flares and primed it.

'Careful!' I shouted. 'Make sure you point it away – no, the other end! Yeah, make sure the back end is pointing away . . . further.'

Ben concentrated so hard on pointing it away from both of us that by the time he pulled the cord the flare was completely horizontal. With a loud whoosh the light rocketed off like a guided missile a few feet off the water. It hurtled away seaward.

We both laughed in disbelief. This was absurd. Here we were; two heavily bearded, nearly naked grown men shooting each other, firing parachute flares flat to the water, about to die within sight of land. I felt a sudden surge of love for Ben. We had endured together and now we were going to go down together in our typically ridiculous fashion.

We would fight, of course. Fight to the end. But now, as the next wave appeared, rumbling towards us with venom, we realised that we were about to capsize again. There wouldn't be enough time to get into the cabin, at least not enough time for both of us to make it. Still, whatever was going to happen, we knew we'd rather be in it together. It was unthinkable that one of us would get into the cabin while the other took his chances on deck. There was no time to vocalise these thoughts, because the next wave was seconds away, rolling grimly towards us.

We had no oars to steer the boat, so there was nothing to do but brace ourselves for another impact. *But what will happen*, I thought to myself, *if we go over again and this time the boat lands on top of us?* This next wave wasn't as big as the first, but still big enough to roll us and I worried that one of us would be seriously injured this time. If the boat capsized it would self-right again near us, so why not jump in on the wave side of the boat to avoid the risk of being injured? In my mind we wouldn't be abandoning the boat, simply limiting the chances of taking a serious knock in the inevitable roll. *Stay on the boat or jump in?* That was the question I was asking myself, and I had about four seconds to decide. Time kindly slowed enough to allow me to appreciate the unattractiveness of both scenarios. Better to act than be acted upon.

'Quick, let's jump in on this side so we're not rolled under the boat,' I shouted. 'We'll hold onto the grab line.'

Ben nodded and we simultaneously launched ourselves over the side. We took hold of the grab line as the wave arrived and violently ripped the boat away from us. We lost sight of her as we were engulfed by the crashing wave then I came up to see in utter dismay that she hadn't rolled. Instead she was hurtling away, carried at unbelievable speed by the relentless power of the wave. A lonely sight it was, glimpsing her surfing off, wildly, uncontrollably, like a rider-less racehorse.

The boat was gone. The sea had tricked us, or had tricked me. Now we were in its clutches, treading water and taking in what had happened. Things had definitely just got worse.

68 The Swim

'A whole hour now passed; gold-beaten out to ages.
Time itself now held long breaths with keen
suspense.'

Herman Melville, *Moby Dick*

We were now in the water in nothing but our cycling shorts. We
were still slightly north of the lighthouse and I was desperately
trying to see the boat that was supposed to be meeting us. In
theory, it would be to the south and through the building
peaks and troughs of swell I tried to catch a glimpse of it.
There was certainly no point swimming after our boat; it had
been carried away far too quickly and would surely be dashed
on the reefs.

'We need to swim for the gap in the reef. That's where the
boat will be coming from, it's just south of the lighthouse,' I
spluttered.

'Alright, let's start swimming. Is your leg okay?' replied Ben.

'Yeah, it's fine,' I said, but as we started a slow front crawl
I felt it aching.

Looking down at it through the darkening water I could
see blood pulsing out in wispy clouds.

'This isn't good, is it?' I said.

'No, this isn't good,' Ben agreed.

We swam a few more strokes and then I saw it.

'The boat!' I shouted, pointing at the white slip that was
dipping in and out of my vision.

'Okay, let's swim hard for it,' said Ben.

We set off swimming a heavy front crawl. Then another roller appeared, crashing and thundering towards us. Now we were in the water the waves looked even bigger.

'Take a deep breath and let's duck under at the last second,' I screamed over the din of water. I plunged myself straight down as the wave reached us, using strong upward strokes with my arms as if I were a footballer entreating the crowd to stand to celebrate a goal with me. I felt the surge of energy above me and came back up in the frothing after-wave. Ben was there too.

'Let's stay close,' he shouted.

We set off again. Then I caught another glimpse of the boat.

'It's there, about two hundred metres away,' I said.

'Tony! Help! Help!' we shouted in unison.

Nothing.

'Okay, let's get swimming, try to stay close,' said Ben.

I was lagging a bit. Dragging my bleeding leg behind me I felt cumbersome and slow. I wasn't swimming properly, wasn't taking breaths as I would in a pool. In training I had often swum four or five kilometres without stopping. *Swim like that*, I told myself and started off properly, taking a breath every three strokes. We swam for a minute or two before I stopped to look for the boat again. Another glimpse. We swam again and another roller appeared. since we weren't wearing life-jackets we could easily get under the waves if we timed it right. We ducked under at the last minute and let the power wash over us. Then there was no sign of the boat. We swam on in the same direction, checking every few minutes, but there was nothing.

'I can't see it any more,' I said, as we stopped to get our breath after the last few strenuous minutes of swimming. We paused, treading water and catching our breath. The sun had gone down and the last grey light lit the sea a dark blue. Ben plunged his head under the water, sweeping it from side to side.

'What are you doing?' I asked when he came up for a breath, knowing the answer full well.

'Just seeing if I can see the bottom,' he replied unconvincingly.

'You're looking for sharks, aren't you?'

'Alright, I thought I saw a shape and you're still bleeding from your leg.'

Then I felt a brush on my leg. I plunged under and round, opening my eyes in the darkening salty blue. Nothing. But I could see the bottom, perhaps thirty metres down. The sight of the rocky seafloor filled me with fear.

'We need to forget about sharks and just swim. If we get eaten, we get eaten, we have to try and make the gap in the reef before it gets too dark to see,' I said. Perhaps my attitude would have been different had I known that Mauritius' most recent shark fatality had happened at this exact point.

'We've only got half an hour before it's pitch black.'

'Alright. I remember from the chart that the entrance is right after the lighthouse, so we have to swim as close as possible to the lighthouse, without getting washed on the rocks but not straying too far from them otherwise the current will push us past the entrance – and we need to do it before dark.'

'Easy. Let's go.'

We set off and after a minute another roller thundered over us. This seemed the biggest yet and I felt sick with a fearful excitement as it bore down on us.

'We have to dive deep!'

'Shit!'

I went under and felt a maddening rush of bubbling water all around. Coming back up into the simmering after-wave, I felt a tugging after-effect pulling me down. I fought back to the surface, spitting out seawater and swearing to myself. This was beyond dangerous.

Then I realised that we had been separated by about five metres. In the building noise and energy of the weather it felt like a long way. I was still behind.

'Next wave, let's hold onto each other so we don't get separated,' shouted Ben.

We swam on and as the next wave careered towards us we clung on together and with a quick countdown disappeared under. As we came up in the hissing water I wondered if the technique helped at all. It felt more like we were trying to drown each other under the wave. But I liked the feeling of solidarity. If we were going down we were going down together.

We pushed on, swimming back out to sea a little to counter the waves, which were pushing us towards the tumultuous water around the lighthouse. We had been in the water for about twenty-five minutes. Now as we ducked under the waves in each other's arms we were beginning to see the comedy of our situation. Somehow absurdity was starting to eclipse danger. Obviously we weren't enjoying ourselves, but we started to joke regardless.

'Can you feel the buzz?' shouted Ben, as we came back up.

Here he was quoting a story I'd told him about Steve, a fisherman friend of mine from Alderney who'd found himself on a lee shore in gale force winds one night. He'd told me he was only frightened by how much his skipper seemed to be enjoying himself, shouting at Steve from the wheelhouse, 'Can you feel the buzz?'

'Oh yeah, I feel it, this is amazing!' I replied, and then, 'Hey, more or less dangerous than Ginga?'

'I think we can safely say this is worse.'

'That wave demolished us.'

'Yeah, the Casios are still working, though. We really should write to Casio if we survive.' We had taken a couple of old-school Casio watches with us. They were the same ones we had worn as kids in the 1980s. They simply had a clock, a stopwatch, an alarm and a light, all for a very reasonable $3.99. As all of the fancy kit on the boat gradually failed during the row we had marvelled at how our Casios had kept going.

Alongside this gallows humour, we were discussing our options and revising our plan. But as our situation worsened it felt important to be laughing as well as battling. We didn't need to vocalise it, but we both suspected at this stage that we were going to die, and if death was imminent it seemed better to go down laughing insanely rather than snivelling bitterly.

Another ten minutes of swimming and ducking and we cleared the lighthouse. Unfortunately we couldn't see the entrance to the harbour through the lines of breaking white water that marked the reef. It was getting properly dark now and the waves seemed to roll at us with a dreamlike slowness until the last second when they lunged, spitting and roaring like a wild animal. As the inky dark was spreading across the sky we said to each other that it was better to try something now rather than be swimming in the pitch black. Although we couldn't see the gap in the reef, we had to get closer and take our chances.

We started swimming in. Still the waves came behind us and still we ducked under. As we made our way in, each wave seemed to get louder. Then, ducking under one wave, I touched the bottom. As I came up I shouted to Ben.

'Shit! I just touched the bottom!'

Before he had time to reply the next wave flung us mercilessly onto the coral reef.

69 The Reef

'Better is it to perish in that howling infinite, than
be ingloriously dashed upon the lee, even if that
were safety! For worm-like, then oh! Who would
craven crawl to land!'

Herman Melville, *Moby Dick*

We were picked up by the wave and rolled over the coral. I
came up waist high, my feet touching land for the first time
in four months. I lifted my feet straight away to avoid the
jagged coral as the next roller was rumbling towards us, barely
visible.

'Quick, we've got to get away from the waves,' I shouted.

We both started to clamber forward, shouting in pain each
time the sharp coral sliced our feet. Then the next wave threw
us onto the coral and as it subsided we found we were crawling
desperately on all fours. As we did the coral broke, sending
us off balance and tumbling into more sharp edges.
Painstakingly we waded, stumbled, crawled and fell our way
forward, thus managing in a couple of minutes to clear the
danger of the breaking waves. Our shrill swear words rang
out, accompanied by the little splash of each fall. They were
behind us now, but we could still hear the regular thud of the
waves. Eventually the pain was too much and, having crawled
about fifteen metres over the barely submerged coral, we came
to a rest.

'Come and sit over here, there's enough room for two,' said

Ben, who was sitting on a brain-shaped bit of coral about a metre away.

I rose on shaky legs and, with my hands outstretched in front of me, started trying to make my way to him like some kind of very badly injured, malnourished gorilla. Feeling the spines of a sea anemone pricking my ankle I quickly withdrew my foot and, losing balance, capsized painfully.

'Ouch! Oh, for fuck's sake!'

'Alright, let's stay put.'

We sat silently for a bit.

'We're going to be okay now. Either we get rescued or we swim the rest,' I said.

'I think I can feel the tide coming in. If the water level rises then we can swim over the coral and keep going to land. I can see the lights on shore; it must be about two kilometres away.'

'We can easily swim that. It'll be calmer on that side of the reef; then we can walk out onto the beach and give some random tourists the fright of their life.'

'We just need to wait for the tide to come in.'

'But if the water level rises then the breaking waves are going to be on us again.'

'How much coral do you reckon is left?'

'I don't know. Looking at the chart in my mind, I think there was quite a bit. I think it's too painful to try and walk over it any further.'

'I've got an idea,' said Ben. He stood slowly and, using a hand to steady himself on the large piece of brain coral, he took off his cycling shorts.

'I'm not sure where you're going with this, but now really isn't the time, mate.'

'I'm going to wrap them round one foot so I can walk on the coral by putting my weight on that foot.'

'Ah, okay. Good idea.'

Having wrapped one foot in the shorts he set off, his wrapped foot edging forward searchingly, like a blind salamander. Having placed it, he then took his next step but landed on some razor-sharp coral. Wincing, he pulled his foot back sharply but then lost balance and fell on his naked backside.

'Arrghh! My arse! Shit! Ouch, that was a really bad idea!' he screamed.

We sat for a bit in silence. The wind was blowing quite hard now and I suddenly felt cold. I noticed my teeth were chattering uncontrollably.

'I can see a light on the horizon,' I said.

It grew larger, until a beam of light was clearly visible. A helicopter!

The whirr of the blades roared as the helicopter approached. We waved and shouted as it flew towards the lighthouse. It started flying in a figure of eight, sweeping over the water where we had originally capsized. Then it started working its way towards where we were. It came close, but the light didn't catch us.

'It's going to miss us,' I said.

It continued sweeping the sea for about ten minutes and then rounded, heading towards us again. Now the beam of light was coming our way.

'It's going to hit us,' I yelled, frantic with excitement.

As the corridor of light illuminated us we both jumped up and started madly waving our arms about our heads.

'Yes! Yes!' I shouted above the din of the helicopter. The light hit us bang on. All around us the water frothed and skidded away as the chopper passed over.

But it didn't pause or alter its path. Instead it continued, meandering back to where we guessed the boat had washed up. Here it dipped down and hovered close to the water. Then it climbed again and, banking, flew back whence it had come. The noise subsided and eventually the light disappeared over the black outline of the island. It had missed us.

Now I felt really cold. I bent over, clutching my leg, allowing my teeth to clatter against each other as fast as they liked. Ben slumped against his coral silently.

I thought of the sad sight of our boat, crippled by the impact of the first wave, lolling in the sea as all our kit and broken oars floated off. The camera was on deck, so it would have sunk. All that footage: the whales, the drill ship, the halfway party and our leaping dorado. All gone, along with everything else: journals, letters and the boat itself. Our saviour and companion smashed by a wave and then carried off by another to be dashed against the reef. *Possessions gone*, I thought to myself, *but remain with best friend and own life.*

'We'll be fine,' I mumbled through my chattering teeth.

'Yes, either the tide comes up and we swim or we have to sit here until tomorrow morning,' Ben replied.

'The main thing is we're going to be okay now; we're going to survive.'

I said this and felt confident, but cold was spreading through my body like venom.

Then the moon started coming up. It was around 7 p.m. and we had first capsized at about 5.15 p.m. It had been a busy day, to say the least, and we hadn't eaten since breakfast. I didn't notice any hunger or thirst, though; the only thing I felt was the cold. The moon was full and the soft light it gave off was reassuring.

'Is it me or can you feel the warmth of the moon?' I said.

'That's just you,' replied Ben, sounding concerned.

'Seriously, I can feel waves of warmth through my body. I think the moon is actually giving off heat. Do you get phantom moments of warmth in early stage hypothermia?' I stuttered, my whole body shaking now.

'Yes.'

'Shit. I think it would be best if we swim, keep moving. If we get the chance to swim are you up for it?'

'Definitely. The tide will come in and we'll swim the last couple of clicks to land and then hitchhike to the nearest hospital, via a bar.'

We sat in silence again for a while, closely monitoring the water level near our respective coral seats. It didn't seem to be moving.

'It'll be my birthday in a couple of hours,' said Ben, who was about to turn thirty-one. The same age as Herman Melville when he wrote *Moby Dick*; the same age Willoughby had been when he steered the *Nereide* into oblivion.

'Oh, yeah. Sorry I haven't got you anything, I mean I did, but it's obviously gone down with the boat.'

'What were you going to give me?'

'I wasn't really going to give you anything.'

'This is going to be some birthday.'

'Would you say this is the worst birthday you've ever had, or are about to have?'

'Not sure. The one I spent by myself in the Sudan was pretty dark.'

As the moon climbed through the sky, I could think of nothing but the cold and of Tory. Somewhere, a few miles away, she would be faced with the prospect of the helicopter returning empty handed. But I had promised her that if I found myself in a life-threatening situation I would fight. At the time I had said it thinking it was only to make her feel better. The past couple of hours had changed everything. I had to stay warm. I had to see her again.

'Shall we sing?' I suggested.

'Good idea. How about a hymn?'

'Okay, but none of your Catholic chanting and mumbling, Stenning. We need a solid Church of England hymn.'

'Don't know the words to any of those. If we sing something that's not in Latin we'll probably go to hell.'

'Wait, a light! Can you see it? There again, a light!'

'It's searching.'

'Okay, after three, let's shout: *HELP*.'

'On three or after three?'

'One, two, three, help.'

'Okay.'

'One, two, three, HELP!

'One, two, three, HELP!

'One, two, three, HELP!'

'Again!'

'One, two, three, *HELP*!'

The sweeping torchlight had now come to rest on us. It didn't move from our direction. Then two torches were switched on, the lights of which flickered and waved about as they started to come towards us. Two people were walking over the reef towards us. We were saved.

70 Rescue and Reunion

'Come a stove boat and a stove body when they will,
for stave my soul, Jove himself cannot.'
Herman Melville, *Moby Dick*

Being English I thought it best to get a quick apology in first.

'Sorry for getting you out on a Sunday night,' I said.

As the two men neared us, their shaky torch beams lit the colourful coral in front of them.

'It's okay, we were watching the Premiership, Manchester United, when we heard two English guys had gone missing,' said one of them with a slight French accent.

'Ah, what was the score?' said Ben, who sometimes pretends to support Man U if they're doing well.

'That, my friend, is not important right now,' said the other guy, who was also French Mauritian.

'Are you injured?' asked the first man.

'We're okay, thanks; some cuts but we're okay.'

'Good, we have a boat this way but we need to get you over the coral.'

'Can't you get the helicopter back? The coral is too painful to walk on,' I said, assuming that these men were the coastguards.

'No, no, we are not the coastguard, they have given up. The helicopter will not come out again. We were watching the football when the man in charge of the yacht club told us two British guys had gone missing near here, so we came out looking.'

The coastguards had given up on us and instead we were

being saved by Thierry, a surveyor, and Eric, a textile manufacturer. Having thanked them, we addressed the immediate problem of getting over the reef. With their trainers on, they tried carrying us but the going was too uneven. So they picked their way back to the speedboat and got some boat cushions which they laid us on and floated us over the reef; Thierry dragging Ben, Eric dragging me. Holding onto the cushion as it scraped over the coral, as my head bumped occasionally into my rescuer's backside, my feelings of relief were eclipsed by a deep sense of gratitude.

'So, we heard you've come a long way to get here,' said Eric as he dragged me along.

'We left Australia one hundred and sixteen days ago and rowed here,' I said, barely believing it myself, it seemed so unlikely.

'Yes, we found one of your oars first, on the other side of the reef, then we heard your shouting. When we saw you with the torchlight, it was a great moment for us, to find you, we were cheering.'

The French Mauritians were incredibly affable and uncomplaining despite being stabbed by anemone spines as the coral broke and fractured under them.

'When the weather is calm we dive here. It's beautiful, so normally we try to preserve the coral but we'll make an exception for you,' joked Eric.

When we got to the boat they helped us in.

'This is the man you should thank,' said Eric, gesturing to a big bear of a man in the boat. 'Fred was the one who asked us to come out looking. This is his boat, and these are my two sons.' There stood two teenage boys gaping in grinning disbelief as if their father had just landed two strange fish or mermen. They gave me a sweatshirt and one of them wrapped a blanket around me.

I watched the wake of the boat as we sped away. So fast, so

easy. Fred slowed down as a coastguard rib came alongside. They exchanged a few sentences in French and one of the coastguard shone a torch in our faces. Then, without another word, the rib sped off. As they disappeared another speedboat came alongside. Hanging off the back, we saw Tony and Ben's dad, who is also called Tony. Ben's dad launched himself onto our boat.

'Are you okay, son?' He embraced Ben and then me and bundled us onto the other boat. We said some hurried good-byes and more thanks to the French Mauritians, promising to get in touch in the next few days.

Now we were on another boat speeding towards the hotel where everyone was waiting. Ben's sister was on board and opened us a couple of Coca-Colas which we downed, savouring the syrupy sugar. Both Tonys were jubilant, grinning wildly and congratulating us on our survival. They told us how they had come out to meet us but got caught in the same weather and had feared for their own lives. As they rode the increasingly big waves they realised that they were only just hanging on and couldn't stay out there without risking capsize. On returning through the gap in the reef, their boat had got stuck on the coral and they'd only just been able to free themselves.

It would have been a long swim, I thought as we sped to land, *but doable*. Fifteen or so minutes later we pulled up to a pontoon and, as the engine cut out, a silence fell among the small group of people gathered. I stepped off the boat and onto the wooden pontoon, searching quickly with my eyes. 'Where is she?' A few meandering, drunken steps forward. 'There!' Then, with another shaky step, I was holding Tory in my arms. This was my best moment, better than the squid, the glassy seas, the lunar eclipse, surfing, whales, stars, better than anything I've ever felt or done before.

Once I'd embraced Tory it became a whirlwind. I hugged my mum and assured her that at no time had we been in any danger. Then I spotted Ben Keith, a great university friend of ours, and his girlfriend, Jo, who had come out as a surprise. They were standing by a homemade banner that read: 'You've only bloody gone and done it!'

Well, just, I thought.

They had their own story to tell. They told us how they had heard about our capsize and had heard from Tony that we'd been spotted in the water. They spent some time worrying before another of our friends, a silversmith called Forbes who was based in Mauritius, had called the coastguard to get an update. The coastguard had told them we were 'safe and well' but would give no further details. Everyone on land had celebrated only to be told, when Forbes called back for another update, that in fact we were still officially missing. They said the boat had been located and thus they'd considered the aerial search complete. Given the wind blowing the palm trees flat and the wildness of the sea, our party had feared the worse.

Standing upright felt odd and I was finding it hard to get used to the lack of motion on dry land. As we stood chatting, various members of staff from the hotel kept coming out to look at us. We obviously cut wild figures with our bedraggled, overgrown hair and bushy beards. 'Viking!' a local guy shouted at me a few days later.

It wasn't long before I requested a Boost and Tory, good as her word, had them with her. Amazingly, as she unwrapped it, some six feet away, I could smell it. The rich milk chocolate scent filled my nostrils; I inhaled the nutty goodness and sweet caramel.

'Oh God, I can actually smell that,' I said.

Ben Keith howled with laughter. 'You've been on that boat far too long. Come on, let's go for a beer.'

'Good idea.'

Afterword

Mauritius

'God keep me from completing anything.'
Herman Melville, *Moby Dick*

Mauritius was a whirlwind of activity. Most of this activity revolved around the hotel buffet, but we also celebrated Ben's birthday and threw a party for our rescuers. With our four-month-old beards and coral wounds we cut crazed figures in the hotel dining area and a few children hid under the table as we hobbled past.

On the first night, a local doctor came to the hotel to put some stitches in my leg. He couldn't get his head around my story.

'So, you were on a boat trip?' he said, threading his needle through my wound.

'Sort of. We came from Australia.'

'You're Australian tourists who went on a boat trip to the lighthouse.'

'No, we're British but we rowed from Australia.'

He nodded his head dubiously. Giving me his card, he told me to call him if the stitches came out.

But the next day he phoned up, most excited.

'I read about you two in the paper, all the way from Australia! A long way to row! You tell them Dr Fakir stitched you up when they ask, okay?'

The paper had carried news of our arrival, but also of the wrangling between the local French Mauritians who had done so much to save us and the coastguard who had given up so quickly. It turned out that the coastguards weren't specialists; they were simply policemen who had to do occasional stints as coastguards and were therefore not well trained. The situation got worse when it emerged that our boat had been looted. The coastguard had recovered her from the reef the following morning, and the boat had been in their custody since. Everything of value had gone, which included thousands of pounds of equipment as well as sentimental items such as the memory cards of film from the first month of the trip. Even the grab line had been cut from outside the boat. What made it worse was that the coastguard seemed to know where everything was. Above all, though, we wanted the memory cards and eventually one of the coastguards said he would make inquiries. The next day he called to say he had them and would give them to us if we gave a favourable press statement.

Convinced they knew where all our other stuff was, I refused. In the end, however, we got the memory cards but nothing else turned up.

Apart from our dealings with the coastguard, Mauritius was great fun. We ate and drank frightening amounts. We played golf and I went back to sea on a boat trip around the north of the island, the place where we were supposed to come in. It was unbelievably sweet to stand in the bow, surrounded by friends, with a gin and tonic, as we did ten knots in pursuit of some humpback whales that kept leaping ahead of us. But it all seemed too easy. It felt like the sea was giving everything up without a fight. Seeing the whales was exciting, and we'd never seen breaching humpbacks on our rowing trip, but it didn't compare to our encounters in the middle of the ocean. They were made special by the contrast, the relief they brought to the fatigue and pain. In

Mauritius there were other boats following, other people screaming and taking photos, and there were other islands and aircraft in sight. When we'd been rowing out at sea there was just us in our tiny boat, thousands of miles from land and from people. After the months of solitude, it felt surreal to be back in civilisation. I have to admit to a sense of emptiness, a sense of anti-climax. Although it was incredible to be reunited with Tory, with proper food and running water, I knew that something else, something very different, had ended. The adventure was over.

Apologia

"'Twas not so hard a task. What I've done, I've willed;
and what I've willed, I'll do.'
> Herman Melville, *Moby Dick*

The crossing times in 2011 show that it was a tough year, at least in comparison to 2009, which is when most of the other successful Indian Ocean rows were completed. The four-man team finished one week behind the four's record while we were two weeks behind the pair's record. Roz Savage, who completed the Indian solo in 155 days, was over a month behind the solo record. In completing the Indian, though, she became the first woman to have rowed all three oceans and she said that the Indian had been the toughest of the three.

To finish at all was an achievement for us. At the time of writing, more than half of the seventeen boats which are taking part in the mid-Atlantic race have been rescued or resupplied.

We could be proud that we finished in 116 days, especially given the failure of our watermaker, GPS and our penchant for lying around in the cabin reading *Moby Dick* on Sunday mornings. The main thing is that we did it. We stubbornly managed to finish, even though finishing meant swimming the last mile.

Meeting a Legend

'This young fellow's cheek is like a sun-toasted pear
in hue, and would seem as musky; he cannot have
been three days landed from his Indian voyage.'
            Herman Melville, *Moby Dick*

Having been on dry land for a few days I chanced to meet
one of the world's most famous journalists, certainly one of
the greatest. I was at the breakfast buffet, loading my plate
with an unlikely array of food, when he approached me in
his wheelchair.

'You've worked up an impressive appetite. Where have you
come from?' he said.

'Well, we've just rowed from Australia,' I said, balancing
some bacon on top of the French toast.

'That's amazing, and can I ask how?'

At this point a striking blond woman approached him.
She interrupted us. 'Come on, Frank, leave him alone.'

There ensued a brief and friendly domestic from which I
extracted myself to eat my breakfast. Once breakfast was finished,
he once again came over and introduced himself. It turned out he
was Frank Gardner OBE, the BBC's security correspondent.
He had been in a wheelchair for the last seven years after having
been shot in Saudi Arabia. In 2004 he had been ambushed by
al-Qaeda fighters, who had shot his cameraman dead and him
six times. But he had gone straight back to reporting and he
still reports from all over the Middle East and beyond.

Now, he explained, despite being on holiday, he was keen to do a story on us. Once a journalist, always a journalist. Not that long after breakfast we went to the bar and over a few beers he wrote the story on his Blackberry and filed it to London. Soon it was among the most-read pieces on the BBC website and messages were coming in thick and fast, many from Frank's colleagues querying whether he was actually on holiday or not.

In the piece, one of the BBC's either very enterprising or incredibly lucky journalists had managed to get a quote from Simon. According to Simon, we were entitled to claim the first unsupported pair's crossing of the Indian Ocean. Having earlier dismissed ocean rowing records as mere vanity, we discovered, on realising that we could claim one, that we were really quite vain after all. Either way our row was officially recognised by the Ocean Rowing Society and our names were added to the website I had spent so many hours looking at during the years preceding our voyage and wondering, dreaming, whether one day we might really be able to do the same.

On the Positive Benefits of a
Brush with Death

'Besides, all these days I should now live would
be as good as the days that Lazarus lived after his
resurrection; a supplementary gain of so many months
or weeks as the case may be.'

Herman Melville, *Moby Dick*

You don't get very far mentioning death at a dinner party. It
remains a taboo subject, despite being very interesting. After
all, it is the only thing that unites all human beings. We
will all die, and keeping this in mind seems like the best
guide to getting the most out of life. Having had my first
brush with death as a teenager, this second encounter came
as a very timely reminder that, like Willoughby, I might
be lucky but I'm certainly not immortal. All in all, the whole
capsize episode was a great experience, physically exciting and
spiritually enriching. I wouldn't do it again, not for any money,
but I'm glad it happened.

In some people's minds the only thing that separates
courage from stupidity is success. I don't think this is fair –
even the misjudged is brave and chance is normally the
governing factor. But if we had actually died on that last day
I would have had little or no sympathy for us. We had chosen
to go, we knew the risks were high and although chaos rained
down heavily on the last day the capsize scenario could have
happened at any time. But with risk comes reward, and our

reward was to cross the Indian Ocean in a tiny boat, to turn our backs on the pettiness and distractions of 21st-century life and be alone on the wide blue sea. For me, the whole experience, even the incident when I was sitting on the bucket and got swamped by a wave, was a privilege. Having so often felt like a prisoner in my own body, during the row I felt the lightness and exhilaration of true freedom. Without the risk of death the ocean would not have been the wild, beautiful, mysterious place it was; it would simply be a controlled theme park and, as such, would probably be as crowded and quietly mundane as any other theme park.

I also felt that in rowing the ocean I'd proved something to myself. I had done it despite my disability; I had done something that would be noteworthy for any able-bodied person. This was important because in our current culture there is a habit of seeing people as victims and understanding them through the prism of what they have suffered rather than what they have done. It's a trap I've at times fallen into. But you can't control most of the things that happen to you; they are, by and large, random. Being struck down by a rare illness is like being attacked by a shark or hit by a bus; it is unlucky and that is it. The only thing that matters is how we respond. So it is with Frank Gardner, who is important and hugely admirable not for being shot but for his subsequent courage, humour and irrepressible pursuit of travel, work and adventure. Although I can't claim any real comparison to the man, I felt that in rowing the Indian Ocean I had in my own way done something more significant than my illness.

The last thing I'd like to say about the rowing, though, is that it was fun. I'm not so desperate to prove a point that I'd do something completely devoid of enjoyment. It was a great adventure and it seemed like a good lesson. What is life if not a sum total of days at sea, trying to stay alive while trying to keep the boat vaguely on course? Before leaving Geraldton, Simon had advised us, 'Stay positive, take care of each other and enjoy it!' This seems to me a pretty good mantra for living life, although I might throw in a few extra words about avoiding bankruptcy and making sure you never run out of toilet paper.

A Lost World

'Yes, the world's a ship on its passage out, and not
a voyage complete.'

Herman Melville, *Moby Dick*

There was one thing, lost in the capsize, that I really grieved
for in Mauritius. The camera in its waterproof case had sunk
without trace, and with it the memory card that held three
months' worth of footage. All of it was gone: the swims
under our barnacled hull, the glittering sunrises, ochre
sunsets, leaping dorado, dancing storm petrels, the looming
oil rig, wild waves, the halfway party feast, the minuscule
sea spider which skated on the eerie calm, and the cavernous
azure of the immense ocean. In the history of things lost,
though, it pales. In 1852, naturalist Alfred Wallace lost all of
the specimens he'd collected during a four-year stint in South
America when the ship he was returning to England in caught
fire. He subsequently spent ten days adrift in an open boat
before being rescued. He managed to salvage his diaries
before the ship went down and his work went on to influence
Darwin's theory of evolution. T. E. Lawrence lost his completed
manuscript of the *Seven Pillars of Wisdom* when changing
trains at Reading, while Gregory David Roberts saw his first
draft of *Shantaram* destroyed in front of him. But even in
comparison, our loss was still deeply frustrating. I'd put so
much energy into something that was now lost for ever and
I couldn't re-create it, not even by rowing the Indian Ocean

all over again. But we were alive and that was the main thing.

In the end I comforted myself by thinking that one day, in hundreds or perhaps thousands of years, the memory card will be found and the people who discover it might be transported suddenly back to another world, a world that may have been lost by then. On watching the footage they will come face to face with a pod of playful pilot whales that once cruised the vast expanses of open ocean and perhaps they will wonder what to make of the two heavily bearded, almost-naked men who, amid all the beauty and the danger, persist in arguing about Celine Dion, toilet paper and in which direction they should be going.

The Final Swim

'We are turned round and round in this world like
yonder windlass, and Fate is the handspike.'
Herman Melville, *Moby Dick*

A few months after our return to England I went up to visit
Ben in north London. We decided to go for a swim in the
Hampstead ponds. As we strolled there we chatted about life
back on land. We got changed outdoors and compared our
fading tans. Soon they would be gone. Shivering in the
autumnal chill, we dived in together, emerging in the fragrant,
muddy waters. As we started swimming out to a small buoy,
Ben turned to me, grinning, and said, 'Well, this is slightly
different from the last time I found myself swimming with
you.'

Acknowledgements

I would like to thank my publishers, Polygon, and in particular Peter Burns, not only for taking this book on but also for his relentless enthusiasm and openness in the process. Thank you also to my editors, Emma Baker and Julie Fergusson.

I should point out that I am heavily indebted in the chapters on the natural history of squid and the battle of Grand Port to the excellent books mentioned below by Wendy Williams and Stephen Taylor respectively.

I need to say a huge thank you to everyone who was involved in the row. There are too many to name here, but everyone who contributed, enthused and encouraged – you have our eternal gratitude. Huge thanks also to our Mauritian rescuers, who either saved us from death or a very uncomfortable night; we were relieved to not find out which.

My thanks to those friends and family who encouraged me to write and gave their time to read this book and share their ideas.

Most importantly, this book would not have been possible without the support of Ben, who generously and bravely let me go ahead and tell things as they were and not in the way that would make us both look best.

Finally, my thanks and love go to Tory: my beautiful wife, lover, best friend, confidante, editor, ally, henchwoman and co-dreamer. I know this book doesn't have any of the boy wizards, teenage vampires or warrior mice that you might have liked, but thank you for supporting me while I wrote it. It's all for you.

Bibliography

Callahan, S., *Adrift* (London, Penguin Books, 2003)

Coleridge, S. T., *The Rime of the Ancient Mariner* (New York, Dover Publications, 1992)

Dawkins, R., *The Greatest Show on Earth: The Evidence for Evolution* (London, Black Swan, 2010)

Hoare, P., *Leviathan or the Whale* (London, Fourth Estate, 2009)

King, W., and Richey, M., *The Wheeling Stars: Guide for Lone Sailors* (London, Faber and Faber, 1989)

Melville, H., *Moby Dick* (London, Penguin Classics, 2010)

Moitessier, B., *The Long Way* (New York, Sheridan House, 1995)

Moitessier, B., *Sailing to the Reefs* (New York, Sheridan House, 2001)

Pepperell, J., *Fishes of the Open Ocean: A Natural History and Illustrated Guide* (Chicago, University of Chicago Press, 2010)

Philbrick, N., *In the Heart of the Sea: The Epic True Story that Inspired Moby Dick* (London, Harper Perennial, 2005)

Raban, J., *Passage to Juneau: A Sea and its Meaning* (London, Picador, 2000)

Robertson, D., *Survive the Savage Sea* (London, Elek (Paul) (Scientific Books) Ltd, 1973)

Taylor, S., *Storm and Conquest: The Battle for the Indian Ocean* (London, Faber and Faber, 2008)

Williams, W., *Kraken: The Curious, Exciting, and Slightly Disturbing Science of Squid* (New York, Abrams, 2011

www.oceanrowing.com